To Susanne —

Confessions
of a
Third-Rate
Goddess

TRAIPSING THROUGH A WORLD GONE WEIRD

BY

Kathy Biehl

The Goddess in me greets the Goddess in you

Kathy Biehl

9TH HOUSE

Confessions of a Third-Rate Goddess

FIRST EDITION
First Printing, 2023

ISBN 978-1-7364321-3-6

Library of Congress Control Number: 2023920056

Book design by Noah Diamond
Author photo by Suzanne Savoy

9th House
P.O. Box 184
Oak Ridge, NJ 07438

9thHouse.Biz

Printed in the United States of America

Confessions of a Third-Rate Goddess

"Kathy Biehl travels from the sublime to the ridiculous on the path to find Mr. Right, and along the way learns to run from both the maddeningly ambivalent to bad Groucho impersonators. And we're lucky enough to join her on the ride."

– HEATHER QUINLAN
author, *Plagues, Pandemics, and Viruses*

"Once again Kathy Biehl displays her blunt & humorous style of storytelling into a world that perhaps seems foreign to some (lawyers, gays, musicians, church goers, and other assortment of characters), but as you unlock these riveting vignettes you may find yourself looking inward as Biehl loudly and outwardly confesses her own past."

– GREGORY G. ALLEN
author, *Cool Side of the Pillow, Patchwork of Me,*
Well With My Soul, Proud Pants and *Chicken Boy*

"Fans of Kathy Biehl's *Eat, Drink and Be Wary* will be delighted to know that she's gathered together a new basket of ruminative and droll essays called *Confessions of a Third-Rate Goddess.* Anything but third rate, the Goddess' travels take us all the way from Houston (the town) to Houston (the street), and from the Lone Star State to the Lower East Side. Naturally my favorite piece contained her unexpected take-down of a one-man dinner theatre show about Groucho Marx, a humorous reminder that Texans have been bedeviling the Marx Brothers since they first played Nacogdoches. A frolicking, rollicking ride of a read. Or is that 'read of a ride?' Let's just call it both, 'cause it is."

– TRAV S.D.
author, *No Applause – Just Throw Money:*
The Book That Made Vaudeville Famous

Confessions of a Third-Rate Goddess

Table of Contents

Introduction

KATHY: *Yeah, my life's kinda weird.*

MATT: *Understatement of the century, Miss Biehl.*

At the end of the 20th century, while television shows and mainstream movies popularized an expensively dressed version of modern adult life (I'm looking at you, Candace Bushnell and *Sex and the City*), a rawer, and definitely weirder, reality was playing out off-screen. My vantage point was inner-city Houston, at a singular and heavily trafficked intersection – collision point, some might say – of young professionals, performing and outsider artists, Unitarians, gays and lesbians, metaphysicians, traveling statues, and beings that defied categorizing. They traversed my life in a blur of sexual tension, ambivalence, and confusion, amid creditable tales of alien abduction, closeted cross-dressing, and an epidemic of clients and friends succumbing to a strange, frightening disease. As previous societal norms disintegrated into the unrecognizable, "nobody could make this stuff up" became the catchphrase for what I witnessed, experienced, and, at times, I confess, instigated.

I coped, in part, by writing. Most of what I saw I chronicled in my zine, *Ladies' Fetish & Taboo Society Compendium of Urban Anthropology*, which flourished from 1988-1998 and gained sufficient prominence for me to be recognized the first time I checked in at Burning Man. I sanitized and attempted to make sense of the universally accessible aspects in mainstream publications like the *Houston Press*, which only led to more fodder for the zine.

This anthology presents real-time reports from the bridge to the millennium, before open gender fluidity, defining pronouns, ubiquitous tattoos, and same-sex marriage, before social media and texting, and before Caller ID and cell phones – access to which would have ended many of these sordid sagas at the outset. As might have therapy. Or psychiatric intervention.

All of this really happened. Nobody could make this stuff up.

A word about language and POV: These pieces reflect a time, place, and, to a large extent, mindset, that no longer exist in the form captured here. If any terms or concepts are jarring, I encourage approaching this work as a historical relic. My attitudes and choices are vastly different now, although I do remain a natural-born magnet for weird.

Goddesshood and other Marvels

Small World

Statisticians may estimate Houston's population at several million, but in my experience, it's 200, max.

Everyone I know ends up knowing everyone else I know. Which is fine, except for a tendency to end up sleeping together, too. Which wouldn't be a problem, if so many of them wouldn't call me to tell me about it.

Some chalk this peculiarity up to the hazard of being an Aquarian, but even for that ilk, my case is extreme.

What set me thinking about this was a recent pile-up of credulity-straining coincidences, none of which, thankfully, involved any dual-supine behavior. My voice teacher had just resurfaced after theater demands had swallowed up his life for four months. In our catch-up conversation, he mentioned that he was moving within the 610 Loop, into Montrose even, into the downstairs of a house next door to a couple of actors, a colleague of his, and an actress/client-friend of mine.

We scheduled a lesson for the following Monday. The next spot on my dance card targeted the same evening, when the assistant director of a just-acquired pro bono client invited me to a strategy session at her house. I agreed to attend the meeting with the understanding that a prior obligation would take me away partway through.

On the double-booked evening, while jockeying for a parking place, I spotted the actress/client-friend who is destined to be my voice teacher's next-door neighbor. She was crossing the street. Her street. Her block, even. After exchanging, "what are you doing heres?" and "what have you been doings?" I told her the address of the meeting. She pointed to the duplex next to her house. The meeting was upstairs. The downstairs would soon house my voice teacher. Our lesson later that evening began with my answering my teacher's questions about his upstairs-neighbor-to-be.

"Not only does everyone you know know everyone else you know, but now they all live in the same block of Bonnie Brae,"[1] remarks my oft-quoted, personal life commentator Rex.

At least these synchronicities have stopped popping up on my street. For a while they were coming to light under my own roof – office as well as home – and I was tiring of the *Twilight Zone* theme topping the playlist on my internal radio.

For example, a friend of a friend heard that a German magazine had assigned me to write a story about the Texas Sesquicentennial. He lent me a book he'd written on Texana and apologized for not being able to locate the manuscript of a chapter on state history he'd just finished for an elementary social studies book. "Who's the publisher?" I asked casually. The house he named at that time employed on its design staff a high-school pal who'd shared my apartment before leaving Houston for New York. I called her. She knew the project; she was designing it. The next

---

[1] As did the editor of the paper that published this piece.

time he dropped by my office, I handed him proofs of his mislaid work.

Imagine these sorts of connections announcing themselves at a social gathering. Increase the number of players, and the intersection of circles can make you downright dizzy. The most engaging entertainment at my Christmas soirees has always been the least intentional – the outbursts, usually mine, erupting as people figure out their links.

The first time this happened, a workout buddy/member of my church was delighted to run into a woman who'd played flute on one of my meditation tapes. I thought he was just hitting on her, but she seemed to welcome the attention. The happy pair announced that a decade before, they'd been back-door neighbors and surrogate spouses following their respective divorces. By evening's end, a second path-crossing occurred – my pal Susan took in the strange realization that the person she'd been talking to for the past few hours had, 10 years earlier, been the best friend of the man she was riding with when a train hit their car and put her in the hospital for six months.

She was more composed at her second Christmas party *chez moi*; this time I reeled. Late in the evening a couple arrived that I knew through meditation and relaxation work; the woman was an occupational therapist who'd coordinated workshops I'd taught at her hospital. Her husband walked up to a member of the Irish folk musician contingent and fell into animated conversation. I searched for the common denominator and narrowed it to the computer industry or Rice University. The therapist clued me in. They'd had the same first wife. "Susan!" I shrieked, running for cover in the kitchen.

I've taken a hiatus from Christmas parties, but as the Bonnie Brae incident demonstrates, this peculiar trait is still dogging me. The reason for it, a psychic has suggested, is that I live at the intersection of a number of light and energy grids. I can't prove that's not true, but I long for a more tangible explanation. The numbers have got to be it. There are only 200 people, and the rest is done with mirrors. Right?

Parallel Universes

The ancient Egyptians had what an art history professor once called "the pancake theory" of reality, which viewed the life-and-hereafter issue as the soul moving through a series of existences stacked up like the breakfast food. A theory like that appeals to a natural symbolist who is also quite fond of food, particularly when covered with syrup. Living with this theory rumbling in the back of my mind for more than a decade has proven it to be good for more than getting laughs at a cocktail party. My tenure in the Bayou City has demonstrated that the theory doesn't just apply to the after-life. It equally well describes the sort of existence that is possible in the here and now in Houston – traversing adjacent but unrelated universes connected by little more than the traveler's paths, without the nasty prerequisite of dying to boot.

Granted, wide-ranging interests play a role in such a journey, and a genetic magnetism for weirdness doesn't hurt, either. But this particular locale certainly helps. Houston provides plenty of raw material for transforming life, with little effort or planning, into a Venn diagram of mismatched sets.

The phenomenon first grabbed my attention a few springs back, when one week's schedule of outwardly normal and respectable events, linked only by the presence of me and flowing alcohol, turned into a passport to the bizarre. It began with a reception for accountants and lawyers, who were treated to serenades by an accordion player on skates, then an improvising saxophonist and accompanist banging on Ozarka water bottles. The ensuing escalation of the unexpected, which included crossing paths with bit players from previous lives elsewhere and, in an unrelated incident, choosing to spin my bike out in gravel rather than collide with the grill of an oncoming car, left me by week's end voluntarily and happily spending time at a wall of machines churning out adult versions of Slurpees.

Just as the pace of life seems to be accelerating, so does this phenomenon. What formerly took a week can now occur in just over a day. Twenty-seven hours, to be exact. Which is what happened with my meanderings through about nine parallel universes over a weekend one May.

The kick-off was an occurrence that is frequent in the generic: the appearance of a major cultural figure, whose presence usually escapes the notice of vast portions of the population. Some luminary or other is always popping through, making speeches, reading works, and breathing the Gulf Coast's refined air along with the rest of us, often before his local renown catches up with the status he has achieved elsewhere. (Joseph Campbell, for example, spoke at Rice University's mid-sized Hamman Hall before a television series and resulting best-seller made him a coffee-table book name.)

This time the attraction was Germany's pre-eminent post-war author Günter Grass, equally famous abroad for his political activism and best known here for a massive tome about a dwarfish child and his tin drum. Academes, one-time German majors, trendy youths, and consular officials in bad suits flocked to the Museum of Fine Arts for the occasion. A change of venue – from an auditorium to an upper gallery crammed with folding chairs – resulted in an incongruous background for the reading. Grass presented observations of poverty-ridden Calcutta amidst dark European paintings in gilt-edged frames.

The incongruity would have been lost on even the German speakers in the audience, however, without the English translations boomed by an actor from the Alley Theatre (a fitting interpreter for reasons in addition to his sonority, since he has portrayed Goethe, the granddaddy of all German literature). Bobbing mannerisms kept Grass' voice, surprisingly soft for one so politically passionate, safely and almost consistently out of the microphone's range; amplification that did manage to slip through was intermittently muffled by the whine of a buffer polishing the floor below (and attendant snickering from certain audience segments with a lengthy shared history of public displays of immaturity).

As any pretext disappeared *en masse* of actually understanding much of what Grass was saying, private conversations broke out toward the back of the gallery. Initially, I'd worried that the reading would bore my companion, a physician whose foreign language training does not include German. Her frustration level was lower than mine; she had amused herself, it turned out, by reading auras. (The speaker's was yellow and white, she reported.)

On the heels of questions about Einstein sticking out his tongue and the improbability of reuniting the two Germanies, we dashed to the indie/art film house beneath the Greenway Plaza office complex, which is always good for visual treats besides what's being screened, it being a spawning ground for new horizons in people-watching. I created an inadvertent spectacle in the parking lot myself, after steering clear of a couple and then recognizing the man as a former boss who'd inspired vivid revenge fantasies. The opportunity to act out a few of them broadsided me instead of him; all I could do was shriek and make anguished hand signals. The level and quality of passion this experience stirred foreshadowed the film we chose: *The Slaves of New York*, a disturbing, if imaginatively costumed, tale of artists with egos in reverse proportion to their talents, and trivial people trapped in dependent, demeaning relationships. For some reason it reminded me of law school.

The pace quickened the next day. It began at the First Unitarian

Universalist Church, which some people have trouble finding because it doesn't have a steeple. (No truth-in-packaging problems here; you could spend months inside waiting to hear a prayer or name of a Western deity, and once you did, someone would be sure to be offended.) With this appointment – rehearsing a baroque opera duet, from Monteverdi's *The Coronation of Poppea* – the weekend's ongoing cultural foray moved into a theoretically higher, if equally non-mainstream, gear. (It dipped sharply back into the camp arena, however, when our pianist took to interpreting his part in a variety of pop styles, probably in a flashback to his last public appearance as accompanist for a female Peggy Lee impersonator.) After our run-through as Nero and bride number two, I joined my singing partner, a man whose upper range exceeds that of most altos, in a visit to a lesbian book store.

Life being but an endless succession of paths that ultimately circle back onto themselves, he departed for the Greenway, while I entered the duplex version of the day's activities – meeting a business client in a converted duplex in Montrose (still a rough and tumble inner-city neighborhood with bungalows and a population scattered over ethnic, economic, and sexual orientation spectrums), then dropping by a party at a duplex in the tamer, more homogenous vicinity of Rice University.

As the number of guests at the party increased, the conversation went from comparing notes on burglaries (which broke out like Dutch elm pollen that spring) to trading tales of chucking prime jobs. Talk of leaving the corporate treadmill may run rampant among the thirty-ish, but these people had one-upped their day-dreaming peers and actually jumped off. (Well, maybe a couple had been shoved a bit.) One was headed back, sort of; tired of battling an amazing litany of diseases she contracted as an elementary school teacher, a former accountant spoke of planning to return to the profession after moving to Ireland – but first she was going to spend months playing pennywhistle in pubs.

Dissatisfaction with the yuppie working world did not stop anyone, however, from demolishing a spread of that world's go-to barbecue. I managed to chug down two helpings before other commitments beckoned. The certainty of weirdness to come lured me away. A test drive of the upcoming Orange Show Eyeopeners Tour was waiting.

This drive was the continuation of a ritual. The director of the Orange Show (not an actual show, but a monument to the fruit) and I have driven and timed the route for every Eyeopener since the tour began three years ago. We've spent whole days reading maps, missing turn-offs, and correcting directions (not to mention trying to make sense of life in these increasingly weird times), all so busloads of aficionados of the offbeat would enjoy a snag-free drive. Even though I'd bowed out from planning this particular tour, I had to go along for the ride.

We blasted off for the Third and Fourth Wards with a typed itinerary and a vague notion of directions. At each stop, Susanne would bound from the car, enthusiastically greet whoever was hanging around, and ask whether anyone would mind if we brought some people by the next weekend, say, maybe a busload or two. No one said no. No one questioned how we found out about their particular little outpost of individuality, much less what two full-figured white girls dressed for extremely warm weather were doing there. No one was rude, or even suspicious, although employees of the graffiti-covered Sundown Bicycle Shop (who were working on the front sidewalk, there being no room inside the roofless shop to sit or move around) claimed they didn't know the owner's last name.

We stopped for a chat with Cleveland Turner aka The Flower Man, who halted his chores to point out the expansion of his garden down the side of his house, a colorful folk art environment in progress down the road from the University of Houston. We walked up to a long side yard filled with towers of stacked television tubes and fans with blades whirring wildly in the breeze, while a powerful distortion-free sound system somewhere on the property was blaring "WAR... What is it good for?" No one was home.

One street in the Fourth Ward yielded some equally screeching brake-worthy spectacles. An irregularly fenced-in yard labeled the O.K. Corral had Western gear tacked to the back wall and hand-painted outdoor furniture with splotchy brushstrokes. (Stunned by its unpretentious stylishness, we both recognized the profit potential if the artist moved his work a few miles west.) A man sitting on the porch put down a bowl of bread and milk to introduce himself as Porter, explained how he built the fence and painted the furniture, and invited us to look at walls he'd painted in his house with the same technique. Susanne ran in; I grabbed her purse from her open car and followed, in time to see her point out to him that his kitchen shared a knick-knack with The Orange Show office: a human figure made of plastic fruit.

Down the street, two men on a corner bench said a chandelier had recently been taken out of the tree above them, but it was hard to tell if anything was missing. The tree and fence were laden with boots, household utensils, and a lot of objects that defied identification.

Its inventory was minuscule, however, compared to a generations-old collection crammed into our next stop, which looked like off-site storage for Texas Junk Supply – recent circus posters, tiny toys glued into printers' boxes, a Day of the Dead altar of skull candles (relocated from a Lawndate Contemporary Arts Center exhibition), vintage Batman merchandise, kitchen cabinets lined with 60s toys and lunchboxes, JFK memorabilia, and

scads of stuffed animals ("real live dead ones," as I once heard a child say), none exhibiting familiarity with a feather duster. The collection's owner wanted time before deciding to allow two busloads to traipse through her lodgings – not so much because of logistics and caution, but because she had been planning to follow some out-of-town friends in a heavy metal band on their Texas tour.

After circling a Washington Avenue gas station reputed to have been designed by John Staub (architect of many a River Oaks mansion), we stopped at the park behind St. Joseph's Catholic Church, which had a wall embedded with tiles made by neighborhood children. I drank from a water fountain built into a giant metal cactus. Our final destination was in the refinery town of Pasadena, a yard stuffed with hand-painted wooden figures and signs. The artist had died a few weeks before the first Eyeopeners committee van descended upon the site. As we drove through a corridor of chemical storage tanks, Susanne talked about the difficulty of trying to convince the woman's heirs that her work was important enough to be documented, let alone preserved.

We returned to the Orange Show with hours to spare before sunset. The wind whipped through the Show's flags in anticipation of the storm that would flood the city the next week. Only one obligation remained for the day. But detours beckoned before I made it home for a breather.

Seeing a friend's car parked outside Munchies Cafe, I pulled in to get a sandwich and give a surprise. The act seemed appropriate, since Munchies operates as an unofficial community center for an odd assortment of hangers-on – classical musicians, folkies, people who read books, and people who want to write them – that blend in an easy-going, comfortable atmosphere. Uncharacteristically alone in the place, my friend and I noted two changes: an imposing dragon sculpture that had just been installed in the middle of traffic flow, and a wooden stall in the women's restroom, replacing one of the sets of curtains that had been inscrutably and inconveniently hung right up against the porcelain. One less reason to drag a man into the restroom, we figured.

What should have been a simple search for camera batteries required two stops, thanks to an unforeseen 7 p.m. rush clogging the closest Walgreens with representatives of every walk of Montrose life. At last, minutes before a torrential downpour, I arrived at a small garage in the Heights for the day's final mission. The task at hand was a private fabric stamping demonstration by a rubber stamp company owner who teaches stamping techniques for Leisure Learning. With a passel of tiny kittens underfoot and a cut glass decanter of rosé within easy reach, we spent the rest of the evening stamping and trading stories.

As I stood next to a vulcanizer (which looks like a device Bluto would have screwed Popeye's head into), storage shelves full of rubber stamps, and muslin kimonos modeled after 16th century court dress, it occurred to me where I had been only 24 hours earlier. I then looked to the future, and it held the promise of a long, recuperative sleep. And a big plate of pancakes.

What's in a Name?

In literary studies it's called metonymy – bestowing a name on the basis of a significant characteristic. In my circle, it's business as usual.

We don't set out looking for nicknames. They occur naturally, in the wake of some unmistakably demonstrative event. Some have stuck well enough to usurp birth names.

As always, this habit runs back to early childhood. My siblings and I had a litany of alternate names for our pets, like "Oh dog who takes up all the room." A lot of non-relatives now inhabit this wavelength as well. One household of friends has a list on the refrigerator of some ten or 20 permutations of their cat's name.

Although often the catalyst, I have a bevy of willing accomplices for these re-christenings. The most frequent stream-of-consciousness-generator was, fittingly, the first recipient. His given name (and I'm not betraying any big confidence here) is Rex, which happens to be the Latin word for "king" and quite common in liturgical music. Appropriately, his true name was revealed to me in the church choir loft in which he and I met. During a read-through of the Poulenc *Gloria*, we came to a section riddled with the phrase, "Rex Celestis."

The concept fit; within weeks one of his baritone cohorts took to calling him Señor Celestis. It also, fortunately, appealed to Rex. At my next office party, he made his own brand of political statement about name tags by filling his with a column of Bible-based choices: "Rex Celestis/Rex Tremendae/Rex Mundi," etc.

HELLO
my name is

This response only fueled the name calling. A medievalist friend and a superb dictionary have since helped me expand the list to include rulership of no end of subjects, from wit and appetite to commentary and invective. (In the process, his *objet d'amour* has, for somewhat hazy reasons, been tagged The Boy Wonder.)

More often these renamings provide a handy way of identifying a person by the role he plays. A late-night chalk scribbling bestowed "Monsieur Musique" upon an enormously talented singer/conductor/composer, who otherwise goes by the same name as a statistically improbable number of significant men in my life.

A name can also venerate and isolate a specific aspect of someone's personality. After a friend made a string of astute predictions about the behavior of a number of people, she started receiving calls asking whether the Oracle was in. A lapsed Catholic/born-again Pagan with a deep appreciation for Roman religious practices has more recently assumed the mantle of "Interpreter of Omens."

Sometimes the process departs from a discernible, rational relationship to the bearer and veers irretrievably into the weird. One of Rex's early creations set the precedent. When a high school friend of mine moved to town, Rex cast about for a way to distinguish this Bill from all the other Bills in my web. He remembered a *USA Today* interview with happy single people, among them my pal and me, which had a photo of our eligible young bachelor displaying a crystal stem alongside his neatly mustached face. In Rex's mind, the Waterford mutated into china, and the newcomer became St. Bill o' the Wedgewood.

The same source also played a role in one widely used label that was never revealed to its referent – a brilliant, witty, extremely outgoing knockout whose charm cut across the spectrum of sexual preference. (A gay friend once roused me from a post-party, hung-over slumber to ask if this guy "knew Dorothy," which confused me greatly because the questioner had a sister by that name. Turns out, the phrase is a euphemism I'd not heard for being gay.) Todd the Gorgeous, a select few of

his admirers called him, or T. the G. for short. It's safe for me to tell you this now because he's left town and stopped writing.

Nicknames also help serve as telegraphic program notes, absurd and inscrutable to those foolish enough to eavesdrop. One night after we'd performed at Munchies, M. Musique began grilling Rex Celestis about the men around me. "Who's Dash Rip Rock?" M.M. asked. "That's Todd the Gorgeous," Rex said, and explained his role in my world. "No, not him," M.M. responded, pointing to another dreamy-eyed blond. "He's her boyfriend," Rex answered. "Who's he talking to?" M.M. continued. "Oh, that's Mr. Largest Hands in the World," Rex answered. The questions ceased.

Not all labels are heartfelt, at least not affectionately. But sometimes the truth hurts. Years ago I watched an acquaintance shift a barnacle-like attachment from one man to another, in a rapid succession that was internally orderly but sent off a backwash of chaos. Once she latched onto a man, nothing could be done to stop her, but the process invariably ran a short course. "She's a nice girl, but she'll go through you like a jalapeno," one observer warned a potential target. My reaction was more succinct. I took to calling her The Virus.

As for me, I have as yet remained unsullied by frivolous nicknames. Some of us just can't be neatly pigeonholed.

Goddesshood Revealed

Speaking of names...

...two more have joined the roster of my titles.

As I walked into a party last fall, I heard my name being invoked two rooms away. The voice belonged to the sole Christian minister in a gathering largely of Goths, *Babylon 5* freaks, and neo-Pagans. All I caught was something about my being a third-rate goddess with shrines in Poughkeepsie, NY and several other cities with goofy names. Sweeping into the room, I took issue with the locations and demanded, "What do you mean, 'third-rate?'"

Hera would be a first-rate goddess, Reverend Jeffrey explained, while a second-rate would be along the lines of Persephone.

"So a third-rate goddess," I butted in, "Would be a goddess in the flesh?"

"Exactly!" he laughed.

Later in the proceedings our host shared chocolate he'd picked up in a duty-free shop. "It's evil," moaned one guest. Rev. Jeffrey elaborated, "It's the best kind of evil." "Evil that can't serve you with a subpoena," I shot back. The minister dropped to his knees and bowed to his newly anointed deity. Everybody howled. Then we went back to the more important business of eating chocolate.

Eating played a role in the other instance of name-bestowing, too, but otherwise the circumstances were at the other end of the spectrum. This one grew out of a rather peculiar restaurant review, which in turn had grown out of one of the weirdest experiences I've had on a review visit.

I went to a place that had swiped the first name, menu, and most of the staff of a wildly (and deservedly) popular, temporarily shuttered business around the corner. Despite the ingredients, something was definitely off at Floyd's on Shepherd, including the shrimp I was served – all the shrimp, in the gumbo as well as in the breaded stuffing. The waitress' blasé attitude suggested this was not an uncommon occurrence. To fill out the column that had to come from this adventure, I visited the icehouse where the real Floyd was serving his Cajun specialties while remodeling the original location. I exercised restraint comparing the two places in print, giving the basic facts without a whole lot of elaboration.[2] The piece ran under the title: "Floyd's and Pseudo-Floyd's."

The pretender's response was straight from the missing pages of a Dale Carnegie course book: try to taunt a critic into a pissing match.[3] Floyd's on Shepherd quoted me in its next *Houston Press* ad: "A plumb [sic] of an experience...fine & tasty – K Beal/Houston Press Pseudo Food Critic."

The first phase weirdly recast my observation that the experience was a bubble out of plumb. The second phrase took the only two remotely positive adjectives not just out of context, but also straight from the sentence damning his seafood. (I'd said the breading on the shrimp was

---

[2] I did not, for example, say, "These thieves tried to poison us with rotten shrimp!" Editors don't like that sort of statement. It invites lawsuits. The one time I did get something suspiciously close to food poisoning after a review visit, my usually laconic editor heard the news with great alarm. "You're not going to write that, are you?" he demanded. Naaah. I don't want to be a defendant, either.

[3] Actually, it's not too surprising given this guy's track record. And the name of his previous business on the site: Richard Head's. Informally, Dick Head's.

"fine" and the stuffing even "tasty," but that the shrimp inside smelled like it had gone bad.) Next to such audacity, misspelling my name was a lagniappe of delight.

No direct action was necessary. One phone call to the *Press* made sure this misquote and my name weren't going to appear in another ad.

Ah, but the paper wasn't his only playing field. The person who'd alerted me to the ad stumbled onto the other: a trailer sign, parked in front of the restaurant, with "'Fine & Tasty' K Biehl PseudoFood XPert" under the name of a dish I hadn't had. Rex counseled a succinct response, on my office stationery: "While you may feel that my culinary expertise is in the area of pseudo-food, rest assured that the license issued to me by the State of Texas is for the practice of real law." I decided to play wait-and-see; surely this guy would get tired of this sooner or later.

It took surprisingly long. Week after week, a new dish came and went above my pseudo-endorsement. I thought up a new letter: "Thank you for not misspelling my name. Now, take it down."

Before sending off the letter, I drove by the place to make sure the offense was still there. It wasn't. A lovely memento of the experience remains: the one-of-a-kind title of Pseudo Food Xpert.

Sticks and stones may break my bones, but names will only help me fill out my calling card, which now reads:

Scheherazade of Weird[4]

Pretentious Socialite[5]

Third-Rate Goddess

Pseudo Food XPert

[4] Courtesy of Dick Freeman, *Batteries Not Included*

[5] Courtesy of a *Zine World* review

Venn Diagrams
of Desire

Amore

It's fall once again, when temperatures and tempers cool down and libidos heat up. The season's disarming pleasantness wipes out the overheated stickiness of recent experience and reminds a person of the occasional benefits of living in a body. Forget the adage that springtime is for lovers. In Texas, the operative time is fall. When one celestial body or another hits the cool autumn sky like a big pizza pie, *amore* breaks out as frequently as outdoor festivals with implausible themes. Not love, mind you; there's no such thing as love anymore. There's only *amore*.

Joining us is our resident relationship expert, whose grasp of the nuances of dating behavior long ago earned her the title, "The Oracle." She lunched with us recently to reminisce about her research into the front lines of postmodern romance.

Tell us about love.

Love doesn't exist any more. It's been replaced by *amore*. Actually there are only two states in life. You're either in *amore* or you're not in *amore*. Neither is particularly pleasant.

Wait a minute – what's this about love?

Love doesn't exist because love is something real and healthy. *Amore*, on the other hand, is entirely imaginary. And so it's everywhere. What we think of popularly as love is really *amore*.

Consider the common phrase "falling in love." Now, one writer has commented that it should be "growing into love" because "falling in love" sounds like falling in a ditch. Well, this is one instance where common parlance has got it right. When you fall in love, you *do* fall in a ditch.[6] You're lying in slime and a snake comes by and bites you and you die a slow, agonizing death. Which sounds exactly like *amore*.

What is *amore?*

Amore is walking on a bamboo pole across a deep canyon; you have banana peels strapped to the sides of your shoes, gale force winds are blowing, and people at the sides are throwing rocks at you.

That doesn't sound very pleasant.

I said it wasn't. *Amore* feels good at first, but you're living in a fool's paradise, population one. (At most, two, if it's one of those rare cases of reciprocated *amore*.) Even the slightest contact with your *objet de lust* thrills you, the victim of *amore*, and you stretch out your enjoyment of each pathetic little incident by playing it over again and again in your mind. It doesn't take long for your thoughts to be completely overrun by your *objet*, who is probably not returning the favor with anywhere near the level of attention that you know you deserve and need, and is thereby assuring that your focus will not waver but only intensify.

What if you tone down your level of interest?

Then you would only increase your own attractiveness as *objet d'amore*. If that's your goal, I'd recommend being a little abusive. Complain;

---

[6] A publicity-shy fellow cynic, on the other hand, contends that the idiom should be "love falling on you," because it's like walking down the street, minding your own business, and an anvil falling on your head.

bark; issue ridiculous orders; call people by the wrong names; don't keep appointments. It is a maxim of *amore* that the worse you treat a person, the more they will desire you.

This advice is hypothetical, of course. You can only do this with people that bore you. If you're in *amore*, you can forget exercising any sort of control over the situation. Once you've fallen into *amore*, your brain is removed and replaced with a unidirectional obsession. You are completely at *amore*'s mercy. And it'll take you to only one place.

And that is?

Let me put it to you in practical terms. Say you're driving down the highway of life and you encounter a sign: "*Amore*: 1 mile." Next to it there's another one and it says: "*Amore* hell: 1.1 miles."

What's *amore* hell?

It's a phone that doesn't ring, broken plans, nights of pillow hugging and watching late-night reruns of sitcoms from the last three decades. Alone. It's having a friend ask you about a cute guy that called her up after meeting her at your party and realizing that she's talking about your steady boyfriend, whose fate would be not-for-very-much-longer if you still had your brain, which of course you don't. It's finding familiar cars in inappropriate driveways. It's nursing an obsessive, irrational devotion to a person who does not return the favor and who would not be worthy of your love – if love still existed, that is.

When you're alone in *amore* hell, at least you have a chance of salvaging some semblance of dignity. In the public sectors, you can forget any hope of retaining the respect of yourself or anyone unfortunate enough to witness your plight. You're just pitiful.

Isn't there any way to stay out of *amore* hell?

Sorry.

How long does a victim spend in *amore* hell?

There's no limit. We've known of one woman who spent a several-year stretch down there, surfacing only every few months or so to check the messages on her answering machine.

And what about when you're not in *amore*?

When you're not in *amore*, your reasoning faculties are intact, you function reasonably well in the world, and you generally regard most discarded *objets d'amore* with more than a faint disdain. Ironically, people who are not in *amore* spend a good deal of time wishing that they were. They usually get their wish. If you're not in *amore*, it's only a matter of time until you are in *amore* again.

Doesn't amore have any positive aspects?

It does lend a sense of drama and grandeur to otherwise dreary little lives.

And there is the food.

Food?

Yes. The *cuisine d'amore*. This is part of what binds the *amore* victim to the *objet d'amore*. Anything soft, gushy, sensual, comforting, or high in fat is food for amore. Italian food is the crown of this cuisine. Especially pizza. If you've shared a pizza with someone, you're sunk. You're already chugging along that old Highway to Hell.

Why pizza?

Think of the anthem *d'amore*: "When the moon hits your eye like a big…"

Oh.

After-dinner drinks are also part of the *cuisine d'amore*. For some reason, Jägermeister ranks high here. Some would-be *objets* have also reported great success with tequila shots.

Are any activities associated with *amore*?

Yes. Cooking together, for example. Chopping and heating and frying fresh, natural ingredients somehow primes the soul for what's about to happen to the participants.

Any places?

There is the concept of the *amore* vortex. This would be a place with a high probability that a person would be sucked into *amore*. A few vortices have been identified that affect the population at large. For example, in Houston, where no one has been observed to be in anything but *amore* since at least 1986, our research has pinpointed Star Pizza, the Orange Show, and the Red Lion as potent, highly active vortices. It is not a coincidence that the last two feature fiery colors. A place like the Blue Moon, in contrast, would not be an *amore* vortex.

Didn't it go out of business a couple of years ago?

You see my point.

I should warn you that it is possible for a specific location to constitute an *amore* vortex for only a small portion of the population. Using Houston again as an example, I can think of an unassuming classical music cafe that one rapid-fire repeat victim could not enter for several years without *amore* breaking out, either within, or because of, her.

Any other glad tidings you'd care to share?

I have two, thank you. *Amore* has a mascot. This is a creature that lives in the dark recesses of the sea, blends into the rocks so passersby can't see it, grabs hold of its victims with steel-trap jaws, and will not let them go. I'm speaking, of course, of a moray eel.

Also, *amore* has at least one amusing by-product. It is not always accurately perceived by onlookers. I call this phenomenon dyslexia *d'amore*. Sufferers of this condition assume two people are in the throes of something hot and heavy when they are not. When a real relationship is going on in their midst, the *amore* dyslexic totally misses it.

Would you care to leave us with any advice?

My best advice is: don't.

But isn't that futile? Isn't amore inevitable?

Yes, and yes.

Who Rewrote the Book of Love?

These are mighty confusing times. More than a few pages are missing from the rules section of the book of love. What's worse, the omissions vary from copy to copy.

I've dabbled in this business of dating for two decades now[7] and don't understand it much more than in the beginning, when I believed that simply thinking hard enough could make my boyfriend call or read my mind. But at least then boys and girls shared common assumptions about how this dating thing was supposed to proceed.

It's hard to read signals when nobody seems to know what game is being played anymore. Some of us aren't even sure we want to be playing the game at all.

Time was, voltage-laden glances and intense conversations meant he'd soon be lunging across a front seat at you. Now it's unlikely you'd be under the roof of the same car in the first place. No one seems to know what to do anymore. What once signaled the courtship dance now heralds ambiguity, ambivalence, and a lot of non-ringing phones.

The longer you're at this, the more what's left in circulation compares to the return shelf at Kmart – crumpled boxes secured with string, shattered objects glued back together so the edges don't quite meet. There's a lot of

---

[7] Reminder from the future: 1990s conditions prevail here.

visible damage. You're probably not looking so great yourself, either.

And those of us who've tried therapy to repair the damage fall prey to problematic side effects. We think everything to death. We want to know the meaning behind actions, words, silences. It's hard to keep animal interest burning with our rational minds in overdrive.

Sometimes I see the hand of God swooping down to keep relationships from forming. An extra-dimensional phenomenon is an entirely plausible explanation for the squelching of one promising flirtation last summer, for example. Through mutual friends I met and hit it off with an intriguing man from out of town. When family business put me in his vicinity, I sent a lighthearted postcard with my host's phone number. He didn't call, for a reason with award-winning originality. I later learned from mutual friends that his fundamentalist brother burned the postcard because a five-pointed star I'd stamped on it marked me as a witch and a Satanist.

Or maybe he was just ambivalent. Everybody else is.

It's easier to forego potentially romantic attractions for the safety of friends; at least with them you know what to expect. (Of course, doing things with friends has a funny way of devolving into a discussion of the very thing you're avoiding.)

But friendships, too, can wander into ambiguous territory. Sexual tensions can seep into the most platonic pairings, when one half entertains long-range schemes while the other has no intention of being anything more than a friend. Gender itself is no longer an indicator of who constitutes a potential romantic partner. Even straight/gay friendships do not necessarily circumvent the nasty little issue of attraction.

Some of us have more experience with this than others. I've been the target of more than my share of gay men's heterosexual fantasies, a frustrating role that began in public school (from the fifth grader who'd pull my ponytail and sing "Rice-A-Roni – the San Francisco Treat," down to my first boyfriend), and has only blossomed now that I live in Montrose. As a result, my homosexuality detector is on constant alert, but even it gets stumped.

One dazzling specimen (in both body and mind) puzzled me and the gay pals I sent to scrutinize him, and it wasn't till I was dangerously ensconced in a disastrous liaison with someone else that the evidence fell unmistakably on the straight side of the fence. Another man quelled my blaring sensors with a several-month course of crush-like behavior and sexual innuendo. Whereupon he off-handedly mentioned he was gay.

Nothing in Girl Scouts or health education said anything about life on the high seas of androgyny and ambiguity, where no one wants to close off any options but no one wants to act on them, either. It makes me seasick, even with my training. It's also made me very wary.

You can't exactly ask a guy whether he's gay.[8] Discreet background checking may answer the question, but even that can backfire. And when the rules are up in the air, most of us revert to the last time they existed, which in some cases is junior high.

I wandered into a weird combination of rule-free and adolescent behavior by asking an older, unmarried friend what she knew about one *objet de lust* with whom we had a common organizational membership. She made a sales pitch instead for another member of the group. I rattled

---

[8] Popping in from the future again, with a reminder about the previous footnote.

off the reasons for disinterest, including something he'd once said that proved definitely, at least to me, that our worlds were irreconcilable.

That night my girlfriend's favorite called to explain and apologize for his statement. My horror increased upon hearing that she'd not only told him what I'd confided, but also given the entire context – including the name of the man I'd been asking about. I rolled onto my back with my feet kicking in the air like a dying bug.

"You've broken the unwritten law of girl talk!" I squawked at my loose-lipped friend. It had been absent from her life for so long that I actually had to spell out for her what I meant.

This drug-free flashback did manage to dislodge overwhelming confirmation of the first man's heterosexuality, which my friend spilled amidst her protestations. ("So he's done the big nasty?" a gay confidant quipped. "As opposed to the big nasty which dares not speak its name.") It also significantly dampened my enthusiasm. I'd taken a hiatus from relationships after swimming the incestuous waters of Houston's acoustic music community, and now the inbred depths of another group had swallowed me before I'd gone on a single date.

Why bother, I wonder sometimes. A lot, actually. The issue seems hopeless. Do things on a purely friendly basis with a man and he'll be the one to ask you how you feel about children. Show interest in a guy and you'll never be alone with him. So I think I'll just stick with my girlfriends.

Then again, maybe not.

Burning Desire

This is not a longstanding, conscious goal. I had to see a couple actually doing it before I formulated this desire. I was sitting at a booth in a ridiculously goofy Hawaiian restaurant, a worthy successor to the tradition of the long-departed Trader Vic's. (That place had a cachet so powerful that a group of Irish musicians kept a flower-shirted vigil there every night of its last week in business, as if to store up mock Polynesian ambiance against a dreary future of non-accessorized drinking.)

The Hawaiian newcomer offered an ideal setting for lounging about on the receiving end of a garish exotic drink with an equally garish paper parasol. The bar was an island adrift in a mural of seagulls, clouds, and foamy tide, against which Don Ho sang away with a happy children's chorus. Beneath its stockpile of Mylar-tipped swizzle sticks and totem-faced ceramic mugs sat a couple who'd opted for the most adventuresome entry on the specialty drink menu. Their straws connected them to a wide-rimmed bowl, big enough to require two hands for carrying, that contained the alcoholic equivalent of the kitchen sink. At the center lept flames.

"I want a man who'll drink fire with me," I said to my companion, who is used to such out-of-the-blue revelations. The thought didn't surprise him; he's heard something about wanting to shoot fire off my fingertips. He responded enthusiastically, and not out of reciprocal interest or even friendly solidarity. He wouldn't mind a man who would drink fire with him, either.

The line keeps returning. Days later I think, "I want a man who'll drink fire with me." I suspect the thought may contain deep meaning. A theory immediately begins taking shape.

It resurfaces during a phone conversation with my accountant. I mention the Hawaiian bar excursion. "I want a man who'll drink fire with me," I tell him, and he roars with laughter, not entirely as a result of the tension from impending IRS deadlines. As I defend the statement, it rises to the level of a Fundamental Truth of my existence.

The concept has now taken on nearly every critical characteristic of the elusive target of my quest. It has fast become my personal Grail.

The image transcends the mere act of sticking a straw in a flame-kissed beverage. It reveals an entire personality. It shows me a complex blend of bravado and flamboyance that makes light of itself, of calculated risk-taking coupled with recklessness and humor, of élan and adventure expressed with panache.

He is a natural showman, skilled in the grand gesture, attentive to appearances without attaching excessive importance to them for their own sake. For that reason, he doesn't take himself too seriously. People can stare and think all they want – He enjoys himself; what matter are the opinions of people who've lost the ability to play?

He's spontaneous and prone to cast off responsibility in ways that endanger no one. However modest his normal habits, my fire drinker is reckless enough to ingest liquids in colors not found in nature, to throw caution to the wind.

But I detect profound depths, too. Drinking fire demonstrates that he is willing to jump into an experience, even if it's potentially dangerous. Even if he risks getting scorched. The act places him within flirting range of the flame as well as of me, and who's to say which could be more threatening?

The risk doesn't daunt him, though. He saunters up to the flame without hesitation. His sharp, agile mind and natural intuition tell him exactly where to place the straw to keep from getting hurt. And, most importantly, he shares the experience with me. We sit straw to straw, on equal terms, growing tipsy from the same source, and, when the last drop is drained, holding our straws over the flame and watching the heat shrivel them into a misshapen residue that will perplex the bartender.

Granted, this metaphor leaves out a few things, like not smoking and not hunting for sport, speaking a foreign language, and being equally comfortable in jeans or a tuxedo. All of those were on a list of a hundred-plus characteristics I actually wrote out a few years ago. (Don't worry; I can't find it now.) Perhaps it is my previous inability to formulate this desire succinctly that has posed the impediment to attaining a Relationship. Naming is a step to claiming, they say.

So here goes: I want a man who'll drink fire with me. You can laugh all you like. Everyone who hears it does. It's a silly idea. And that's why it's so appealing.

It makes me laugh, too. And I'll still be laughing when you see a flaming bowl between a pair of self-possessed characters engrossed in mirth and each other. Look for a woman with a raised eyebrow and a mysterious smile. That'll be me.

Fan, Male

My sporadic column in the Houston Press *drew fan mail from four men, all of whom I ended up meeting and none of whom I care to know any better, socially or otherwise.*

The Straits of Ambivalence

Be careful what you ask for

Seeing a couple drinking a flaming volcano prompted me to quip that I'd like a man who'll drink fire with me, a concept that I stretched into a several-hundred word essay for the *Houston Press*. One application for the position arrived at the *Press*, in the form of a letter.

The writer offered to drink fire with me with stipulations ranging from my taking the first sip (to show I'm willing to feel pain), to meeting age and appearance criteria (including the size of my ass, his word), to asking him nicely, maybe begging or whining. He threw in a few compliments, a description of himself fit for a dating profile, and suggestions to talk, meet, maybe drink some fire.

I spotted the early warning signs of assholedom but hell, I was bored and meeting this guy sounded like an adventure. Maybe even essay fodder.

My editor read the letter to me over the phone and put it in the mail. Before it reached me, he was calling, demanding to know why I hadn't phoned him yet. In our first meeting, under the sensible circumstances of lunch, he imparted a few crucial facts – he was just off a 13-year marriage, during which, he claimed, he was the only monogamous man in the United States (a status he had a stated interest in obliterating); he had an agent shopping his novel (which pivoted on the rape of a female politician; his published work covered a trial convicting a man of bludgeoning his wife to death in bed), and was eager to see my writing go further than a local weekly; he'd just moved here to make commercials for a local consortium of Brand X car dealers; and one of his first jobs here featured an actress well known to me as a friend, client, and, isn't it a small world, subscriber of my zine. He asked me point blank if I were gay,[9] because, he insisted, he needed to know right there and then. After a string of wishy-washy guys, I found such straightforwardness – well, let's be honest – gall – somewhat refreshing. The message came through loud and clear that this person was not Relationship material, which was not what I had in mind. What I failed to see was that they were not even the makings of a fling.

We got together a few times over the next couple of months. When he picked me up for our first date, the radio in his non-Brand-X car was playing "Fire" by The Crazy World of Arthur Brown; on another evening, he threw the I-Ching and got the hexagram named after the same element. He was witty and entertaining and emanated a constant

---

[9]Would someone please tell me why this question keeps cropping up?

sexual current that was intriguing at first, but quickly vastly disconcerting. It was also clear that our world views were so at odds that mine unnerved him completely. He took to calling me Samantha, asking if I could twitch my nose, and admitting repeatedly to a vague concern that I was going to make his penis fall off. (He got that idea on our first date, which had devolved into his demanding explanations and demonstrations of my various occult inclinations. Feeling more than a bit like a small animal being mauled in the jaws of a pit bull, I had lunged for the time-honored approach of heading detractors off at the pass and admitting to the worst before being accused of it. My ill-chosen label for my metaphysical work did not prevent him from offering me, that same night, the opportunity to get acquainted with the very appendage he would later, at least verbally, seek to protect against my perceived powers.) (I declined.)

On our second lunch date (during which his disheveled impression suggested not having shaved that morning or slept much the night before), he announced that he decided he didn't want a physical relationship, pointed out that I had stopped chewing my food, and asked, "Are you disappointed in me?" as he rubbed his hand up and down my arm. It was a rare moment of speechlessness in a life of constant chatter. Gall was losing its glamour.

The common denominator of our remaining phone calls and meetings (hey, he was straight, I hadn't been out much in the previous three years, and this was a novelty, okay?) became his demanding reassurances that it was fine if we were just pals, because that's what he really wanted right now, and then acting phenomenally provocative. He kept asking me out – for drinks, for home cooked meals, even for – at his insistence, not mine – the sidelines of the Gay Pride Parade. I maintained a reactive attitude toward the situation, which meant I didn't initiate contact or invitations. The one time I deviated from this policy, he broke the date, disappeared for a week and a half, and reappeared in search of a shoulder to moan on. Over the course of 11 hours, several shared pitchers of margaritas and strawberry daiquiris, a couple of beers, and five to seven tequila shots each, he spilled out an anguished tale of an atomic lust bomb having just detonated between him and the owner of a PR firm who was about to move in with a long-time boyfriend and had become the most desirable woman in the universe to him, the Firedrinker, first (a) because she put off going to bed with him for a week after they found themselves playing with each other's hair at a trade luncheon, and then (b) because she put the brakes on the affair. The reason for "slowing things down" – this is a less than 10 day period from meeting to braking we're talking about here – was, all parties later learned, that the man she was about to move in with was not just her boyfriend, but her business partner. I took my cue, finally, and bid the Firedrinker happy trails.

Eight months later I saw his name at the bottom of a letter to the editor of the *Houston Press*. The letter praised an article investigating a plastic surgeon infamous for breast implants, disputed the notion that all men are hung up on breast size, and asserted that he'd take a 36A any day over a D cup with no brains. My response was pithy, organic, and bi-syllabic. I clued my *Press* editor in on the writer's identity and was told, after the howling died down, that she'd edited out an extremely angry sentence about his ex-wife and all her girlfriends having had breast implants.

Time to lock the door on this chapter and finally return those books he'd lent me, I decided. On a Friday the 13th, my tall, slender, long blond-haired receptionist (two other people also applied for the delivery person position, one gay and one lesbian, but this particular physique seemed most appropriate for the task) hand-delivered to his advertising agency a manila envelope containing a black lace 36A bra tied around the books and bearing the typed note: "heard you preferred this size." Both delivery woman and chauffeur hot-tailed it from the driveway, and a friend elevated me to the rank of Imp Diabolic. I still get physically nervous over what I have done and even now cannot believe I am typing it out for you to shake your head over.

Three months later, which brings us up to about a year after this idiocy began, a friend's boyfriend mentioned that he sometimes drives vehicles in commercials for Brand X dealers. The web asserts its omnipresence again! I asked if he's worked with the agency's creative director. The response was immensely gratifying. "You mean that womanizing little chicken shit? He's a tit man."

The Houston Press' *publication of "Who Rewrote the Book of Love?" struck a deep and disturbed chord that drew letters from three men, none of whom saw fit to leave their praise at one communication.*

He's Just a Boy Who Cain't Hear "No"

Psychiatric assessment: repressed homosexual;
worst case of narcissism ever encountered by one friend's therapist

The letter seemed innocent enough. It was typed, intelligent, witty, and even philosophical. It set out a companion theory of an epidemic of emotional unavailability among women (in Houston, at least; he'd just moved here from the Midwest), and suggested that the two writers might discuss their theories further. A sense of humor, some modesty, and bemused bafflement shone through. They proved to be apparitions all, a sorry fact I did not suspect when I phoned the writer one evening.

"Sherwood Forest," he answered the phone. That was the first of only three things he would utter that would make me laugh. (Two others would trigger unprecedented roaring, the final time of a frighteningly nasty, disbelieving nature. But we're getting ahead of ourselves.)

He immediately revealed a most acute propensity for repellent puns, and almost as quickly admitted, without prompting, to membership in Mensa, a love of barbershop music,[10] and extreme rigidity in the department of personal scheduling (taking a nap every day after work and staying up late to watch reruns of *Hill Street Blues*). Within minutes he read a carefully compiled profile of his perfect mate: a tall, blonde, tanned, college-educated, Jewish couch potato who dresses like a beach bum, has a sick sense of humor, and doesn't eat chicken fajitas because the stench of the grease and onions stays on your skin all night. Did I fit? he asked me. Nope, not even five percent, I answered; I'm not your woman. He revealed his bottom line: alive and breathing. Still no go, I dissuaded him. Did I have any girlfriends who'd date a man who knows how to "keep his hands to his cotton-picking self?" I offered instead to assemble a panel of women willing to discuss his complaint of emotional unavailability.

That was your first mistake…

He agreed.

This gathering was clearly a job for the friend who earned the title

---

[10] Before you take offense, and we know who "you" are, consider this: barbershop music is the only activity in this man's life, besides first-dating. It comprises his entire record collection, except for a disk of *Carmina Burana*, and forms the focus of his vacations. Nuff said?

Lady Susan O' the Vortex (because of the frequency one would break out inside or around her). Another single pal signed on, as well as a married journalist who smelled cheap entertainment in the making. The proffered physical description of the writer turned out to be true: 6'4", dark-haired, and indeed a model's body. Cowed by so many women, its inhabitant didn't talk much, except to (a) emit pun barrages of hostile, conversation-defying levels, which slowed only after the group repeatedly, communally yelled at him to do so, and (b) identify himself as (I) extremely bitterly divorced and (II) small world! the cousin of Susan's last housemate. The meeting adjourned after a few hours with no promises whatsoever on the part of any of the women.

A weird pattern ensued: mechanically spoken phone greetings or messages suggesting getting together and urging me to refer candidates for dating. My response was equally predictable: declining both requests and making brief, polite, but distant conversation, except in the case of answering machine messages, which I did not return.

Two or three months later, I suffered a lapse in judgment and told him about a performance of mine at a classical music club. He was one of the first to arrive and last to leave. My stupidity was topped, however, by Susan, who not only sat at his table, but actually talked to him as a sympathetic fellow divorced person. During intermission, she cornered me in the restroom: He had said I had a body that would make a bishop kick out a plate glass window (Hence laughter outburst no. 2). He later repeated it, shamelessly and proudly, to my face.

This opinion did not stop him from homing in on Susan and pressuring her into agreeing to meet him for a drink on the express terms of friend. The agreed condition did not stop him from trying, but failing, to transform that appointment into dinner and later pressuring Susan into dinner on a second evening. Whatever the personal cost she may have paid, her brush with him did provide a fascinating eyewitness report of his apartment. A bookshelf tells so much about a person, and his book collection, at least what he showed her, was filled only with trendy self-help guides. After seriously claiming prowess as a chef, he proudly showed off the contents of his pantry. Cans and cans of Spaghetti-Os. Cases full, maybe 75, Susan estimated when she called to moan about one of the weirder evenings in her extraordinarily bizarre dating career.[11]

She wasn't the only one moved to moan to me. His little bachelor's heart didn't know whether it was love or not, he cried out to this unwilling monkey-in-the-middle. What did I think? He asked. I saw the need for crisis intervention and abandoned a long-standing policy of non-involvement. I played up the short life span of Susan's previous, ummm, entanglements. He moaned. Months? He whined. Weeks, I insisted. He moaned more. Then he asked me to keep an eye out for women to date him. No offense to my friend or anything. Would I go out with him? I declined on all counts.

Around this time, ads in two different personal columns sounded suspiciously like this guy. "Model's bod, Mensa mind" began one, while "world class kisser" led off the other. My advisers independently concluded he'd placed them both. Only Susan turned one of his continuing phone calls into the opportunity to confront the source and obtained confirmation. Yup. He was startled that we had recognized him. Why was he getting such a feeble response rate? Susan had a few ideas and agreed to meet him for a drink, expressly as a friend, to pass them on. No judgments as to why she willing crossed paths with him, okay? Slack will be given.

WARNING: THE REMAINDER OF THIS PARAGRAPH

---

[11] Don't challenge this assertion unless you're ready to have your concept of reality sorely tested.

MAY OFFEND SENSITIVE READERS. LIVING THROUGH IT CERTAINLY DID US. He took the meeting as an opportunity to disclose a sexual dysfunction, despite her protestations that she didn't want/need to know: He doesn't come during intercourse because he was taught to jerk off the wrong way.

Let's break this down step by step: How much more angry and hostile toward women can you get short of, say, bludgeoning them to death in bed? "Was taught?" Where exactly are these lessons offered? By whom? "The wrong way?" What's that maniacal laughter off in the distance? You got it: it's outburst no. 3.

Once Susan got him off the subject, she spent the remainder of their time together telling him why women weren't answering his ads and why she wasn't going out with him. He inquired about the possibility of my going out with him, which she pooh-poohed. After this, he walked Susan to her truck, let himself in, and tried to jump her bones.

Meanwhile, every few weeks or so my answering machine would disgorge his mechanical, identical message. The few times he caught me at home, he'd slip in reports of his recent dating schedule (always first dates, no repeats) before I'd truncate the conversation. The message changed in mid-fall, at the insulting time of 10:30 on a Friday night – say, what he'd really like to do is step out some night with a foxy woman and how about it? Name the activity, as long as it doesn't cost much, and by the way, here are some dates that he's available, followed by just about every weekend for the next couple of months. My male behavior consultant known as Ask A Guy counseled responding that I was dating a DEA agent. Or suddenly engaged. He even offered to pose as Officer Ask A Guy, outraged that this jerk was bothering his fiancée. I continued ignoring the calls. The only follow-up phone call that coincided with my presence came late during a dinner party. My house was full of men, all of them gay, and one of them did me the favor of answering the phone.

This development pushed the man into other media. A few weeks later, a fax arrived at my office announcing that the The Committee of People Who Think Kathy Biehl'd Make a Pretty Good Companion (being a committee of one) had awarded her an evening in the cultural activity of her choice, no strings attached, with an unmarried man guaranteed to be heterosexual, being ta-da! Guess who? The list of possible dates included New Year's Eve. I set the fax aside for inclusion in my zine but it disappeared in transit, into the rarely-tidied regions of my car, from whence it surfaced after New Year's, before disappearing again. I ignored the fax. Two weeks later the man who'd been singing on stage with the potential temptress of bishops reported to me that a man had just called him at work to ask, "Does Kathy just not go out?"

An unprecedented quiet followed, till one February evening when my friend John was treated to the rare sight of me falling to my knees, pounding a table, and screaming, "No!" as the answering machine played a seemingly innocuous message from a man with a really strange name. The only time since then that he has succeeded in catching me on the phone – with an inquiry about my music – led to the calculated decision to profit e'en e'er so slightly from this ridiculous situation. I told him about my cassette recording. He ordered one. Payment was enclosed in a letter that contained an elaborately worded plea for me to refer two or three emotionally available female prospects.

Hunh?

The Man of Letters

Join us now for a change of pace, that rarest of occurrence on the High Seas, a sweet little tale, and a bittersweet one at that.

Fan letter two was incisive, reflective, amusing (comparing his thinking to a cow's digesting), deferential, and politely presumptuous enough to suggest I read a couple of specific short stories. It ended with a postscript assurance he was harmless.[12] Fortunately, he was telling the truth. The letter was the first of 20 I would receive in seven weeks.

My first response was brief. His return volley began with switching from bovine similes to Marxist salutations ("Comrade"). It peaked in a description of anti-Papist Klan art at the Houston Gun Show that revealed a refined knack for spotting and conveying those weird cameos to which my zine was devoted. His next letter described the contents of his desk, unearthed during an attack by the gods of order, and enclosed one of the findings: a particularly threatening chain letter. A postcard, also unearthed, soon followed.

He painted himself an introvert who preferred to keep his communications at a comfortable distance. By the fifth letter (sent on

---

[12] My inclination was to write back, "P.S. I'm not." When I finally succumbed to it, his response was speedy: "Of course not; you're a lawyer."

New Haven Holiday Inn stationery), he addressed me by name, revealed his employer (a university), his philosophy that crazy ideas should not be dismissed too quickly, and a confession of his own recently crazy actions: using the U.S. Postal Service to insinuate himself unobtrusively in my existence, regardless of the probability of failure, which he conceded was high. His assessment of my probable personality, based on my published essays, got my attention: Intelligence; independence; good sense of humor, with a readiness to laugh at myself as well as the world; ability to endure painful times without losing my marbles or my spirit.

I started asking questions, in writing. He dribbled out answers carefully. By this time the office staff had come to recognize the handwriting, and each new letter was read publicly for the enjoyment of the secretary and clerks. Letter six said he'd been compared to beat poets of the fifties, except he likes iambic pentameter too much. Letter seven, addressed to Most Honorable Madam Prof. Dr. Biehl, advised that he should be approached as "Reverend," having obtained ordination in the mail. Letter eight discarded the "You are what you eat" approach in favor of disclosing the correspondent's favorite games: playing with the minds of his brother's children; sending acquaintances preposterous definitions of their names. A mid-sixties b&w photo of four boys, obviously brothers, accompanied the ninth missive, which laid out a series of stories of things that had happened between them, and strange thoughts that the youngest had had.

The 10th, penned under disability of jet lag and extreme sleep deprivation, detailed his just-completed attempts to get the stove lit in an apartment outside of Paris. The six ensuing letters from France finally disgorged his occupation: mathematics professor, with a security clearance and defense department work to boot. The two correspondents took to trading tales of bizarre childhood incidents where intellectual maturity outpaced the calendar, of academic life as a whiz kid and otherwise, and of wandering observantly through foreign lands.

I found it all pretty interesting indeed and appreciated the "no fuss, no muss" aspect of limiting contact to correspondence, especially in light of a disgusting melodrama that was brewing in my, um, social life. When he enclosed a magazine horoscope and joked about the apparent ominousness of Saturn traveling through his ninth house, I took it upon myself to explain to him just exactly what that meant. He carried out his promise to light a candle in honor of the Society at Notre Dame, but the notion that his idolized correspondent has lent her intellectual powers to astrology lodged firmly in his scientific psyche. His salutation returned to formal, though he did devote nine amusing pages to the subject of haircuts, and a letter almost as long to explaining his insistence on walking everywhere in Houston, an almost unpatriotic way of being in this car-crazy clime.

Needing benign distraction, I threw him out a dare. I told him a day, time, and place that I would be with Lady Susan O' the Vortex. He could come or not, as he pleased, and look for the woman drinking Negra Modelo. I spotted him as soon as he walked to the door, but gave him time to find me. He was tall, slight, bearded, and barely 30; he spent easily 20 minutes carefully eavesdropping before coming to our table. His speech was even more serious and philosophical than his writing; what came through most clearly was that he was that rare creature, a genuinely nice but painfully shy person. This person would be an interesting friend, I thought. He was thinking something else. He stopped writing.

Did the real me so jarringly not match the imagined? I wrote. What startled him was the astrology, he admitted, but then, I probably hadn't expected him to be connected to the military, either. Well, no, but I subscribe to the SubGenius tenet that slack will be given. The letter's final paragraph appealed to me. It noted the luxury of summer fading into the distractions that accompany the school year, and looked ahead to dreaming

of the semester's end. It would make a nice end to this chapter, I thought.
I did not write back.

Office mail would never be the same again.

How to Win Friends and Influence People[13]

Psychiatric assessment: sociopath

The least interesting response was a letter scrawled on the back of a
Merchant Marine newsletter. The author praised the piece, suggested I
would have better luck with men in New Orleans, and admitted he might
have been married 30 times over in the past decades except that lust, not
love, had been the order of his day. The signature rang a bell. I traced it to a
man I'd talked to once at a screwball comedy screening at Rice University.
He'd been sitting next to Ms. N, an acquaintance of mine from church,
and had asked me to photograph the pair during intermission. By his
scrawlings, he obviously didn't link his one-time photographer with the
essay author. Nor did he later match my writing identity with my singing

---

[13] It's Opposite Day!

Unitarian persona, and several months later carried my guitar into a club for a gig still oblivious to all the whos I was, am, and will be. Something told me not to clue him in.

Ten months after the essay appeared, he phoned me at home to see if I, the person listed in the church phone directory, was also the author of the essay he'd liked so much. I begrudgingly confirmed his tardy conclusion. What made him connect me to it, after all this time, was that he had been looking over his outgoing mail log and found my name listed as the recipient for the fan letter. He'd compared that name against the ones in the church directory and the *Houston Press* masthead and finally realized that they were all the same. He recounted all the times he'd seen me at church, including a few I'd blanked out – such as when he'd allegedly followed me to my car and I'd shot him a hurried and harried look that made him decide, "This woman must have a problem with hostility."

"But talking to you over the phone is easy," he exclaimed, and announced that he was going to call me again! "Please don't," I begged and, sensing the absence of any regard for appropriate behavior, added, "Don't call me at 4 in the morning." He wouldn't ever do that, he said, and quickly made it clear that being considerate of any needs other than his had nothing to do with it: he gets up every night at 2 to write, and 4 is when he quits and goes back to sleep.

Within a few days, a note, scrawled across another newsletter, appeared at my home address. This one had two paragraphs, each about a woman. Ms. N, he said, had told him only that I was a church member and must not have known I'm a writer. He gave the years they had dated, with a parenthetical that she got tired of being a mother figure. Ms. X, on the other hand, he'd dated for eight months, but stayed out of her bed because she was into control and dominance.

Ask A Guy was stunned by the audacity and presumptiveness of this letter. I chalked it up as par for the course for unattached men in my congregation (who had inspired the metaphor, in the essay in question, likening the walking wounded to banged-up boxes on the return shelf at Kmart.)

Everyone I know being caught up in the same sticky web, I recognized the name of the second alleged girlfriend. Ms. X is not only known to me, but a member of my women's circle, yea, even a subscriber to my zine. The letter's contents were reported to Ms. X, of course, who clarified two points: This man stayed out of her bed because he was never invited into it, and her "control and dominance" consisted of suggesting, after he'd become put out at a waitress, that they (a) stay at a restaurant in the interest of saving time and (b) share dishes of Chinese food.

Within a week, the Merchant Marine left a breathless answering machine message that if there was a movie at the dollar cinema I wanted to see he'd take me but if I wanted to go to another movie I'd have to pay my own way. Something told me – a backlog of coaching by Ask A Guy, perhaps – that calling him back to say no would be interpreted as a sign of interest, so I kept my silence.

Within three days a note arrived, again on the back of a newsletter. Single Houston women do not return phone calls from single men, he had noticed. If returning his call (date of call included!) was difficult, I could talk to his answering machine between 7 to 11 on weekdays. I would have to actually speak, he cautioned, and not merely breathe hard or remain silent, or he wouldn't know the caller is the one who writes like a sacred bard.

This one infuriated me. Ask A Guy counseled direct confrontation as the only solution. I didn't want to call my pursuer and was strangely relieved to be freed of the task by running into him at Kinko's. He greeted me with a manic grin. "I got your letter," I said. "I thought the level of hostility was out of proportion to the situation, and that's all I want to say about it." "Oh," he said.

Again within a couple of days, I got a letter, this time on a card. He'd discussed our conversation with a friend who thought I'd left things open. His earlier letter was confrontational, not hostile, intended to provoke a response, not stifle one. Because of my nightclub and newspaper affiliations, he'd thought I was a "seasoned hoofer with a track record," so he had no clue I was so sensitive, and apologized.

The exchange stands as proof that our world consists of several intersecting planes with the misleading appearance of being one reality.

The Sally Rogers Syndrome

Straight men divulge what makes a woman "one of the guys." For real.

A couple of years ago we infiltrated enemy lines and found a man willing to speak – to women, about men – without being tortured: our resident male-energy expert, Ask A Guy. Recently we stumbled on a couple more who are open to shedding light into the straight-male psyche, or at least to letting us buy them a beer.

Joining Ask A Guy are guest Guys, King Leer and Sensitive New-Age Guy.

These are real people. This conversation really happened.

KATHY: What I have convened you for is to discuss the Sally Rogers Syndrome. She was a character on *The Dick Van Dyke Show*—

SENSITIVE NEW-AGE GUY (SNAG): Rose Marie?

Yeah, the woman writer who is always "one of the guys."[14] I would like to hear, first of all, what a woman does that causes her to be treated as "one of the guys."

ASK A GUY (AAG): Well, you have to preface that: Does she want to be treated as one of the guys? Or is she trying to be one of the guys? Because, like in our work situation, we have a lot of the secretaries who want to be

---

[14] Who pined for the really dynamic, attractive men but only got asked out by Herman Glimmscher, remember? We do. Sigh.

one of the guys.

KING LEER (KL): The will to be a guy.

SNAG: And I think being able to fart and spit helps.

I mean from your point of view. If you walk into a situation, what sorts of things does a woman do that causes you to then conclude that she's one of the guys?

AAG: Her language. If she cusses…

I'm dead.

AAG: The topics of conversation…

SNAG: I think a certain ease around men. Women who aren't trying to put on a front all the time around you.

AAG: Well, you can see right through it.

KL: I think it's the things that aren't there that really clue you in. It's all the mating behaviors that go on.

AAG: Women that tell dirty jokes are one of the guys.

KL: It's the verbal equivalent of shoulder punching.

AAG: You don't have to talk sports, you don't have to talk politics, you don't have to read the sports page and regurgitate that to be one of the guys.

SNAG: I can think of a few women in particular who are very much considered one of the guys in their circumstances and they abhor sports and they make a point of not needling guys about spending too much time on it. But part of it is not showing any particular sexual interest and being relaxed and not putting up some sort of a front that says, "I don't want you to know the real me."

KL: A coyness.

AAG: And not easily embarrassed either. Somebody could say something to her, somebody could say almost anything to her and it wouldn't faze her. On the outside.

SNAG: She's not gonna regard it as harassment or as some sort of obscure testing that's going on. To me I think the word that sums it up is relaxation.

KL: The first person who has to accept her as one of the guys is her.

SNAG: It's not so much wanting to be one of the guys; it's just already feeling like one of the guys. I think women who are that way like guys. And they're not carrying a lot of preconceptions, a lot of excess baggage with them into dealing with guys. They'll talk with you pretty much on your own level and for whatever you are. And they also don't get bogged down in a bunch of stuff. If it's time to go, they'll cut it off – "Yeah, listen, I'd love to talk to you but I've got more important things to do" – in a way that a guy can do, you know?

SNAG: She's not playing any of those roles like the mother or the sister or any of those sorts of things.

AAG: Or trying to play emotional games with you. She's not trying to trap you into anything or trying to hold on to you in some way. It's more like, again, a masculine behavior: "Look, it doesn't bother me; let's go onto the next subject," or, "I don't have time for this." A lot of people who have emotional behavior, they start and their emotions come out. They start dragging things out, and guys are going, "Get away from this."

KL: There's less subtext between one of the guys.

AAG: When a woman is one of the guys, you can easily tell that she's not putting on false pretenses. With the girls that put on the false pretenses, you feel the defense mechanism coming up in between you. It's like I've got a wall in front of me.

SNAG: The role playing that's going on –

AAG: Right. "This is the face I want to outwardly project, which is something different from what I am." People see through that.

SNAG: So Kathy, are you one of the guys? Is that the problem here? You're altogether too much one of the guys?

KL: Hit rewind.

AAG: And then you have the problem with the girl who's one of the guys that the guys don't want to get involved with.

That was my next question. But actually, I wanted to know, how you decide when to treat someone as one of the guys, and then the next step: Once you realize that a woman has been pigeonholed into that, is there anything that can be done about it?

KL: Find a new group of guys.

SNAG: Absolutely. That's the only way.

AAG: I agree, too.

So you wouldn't get romantically involved with someone that you had treated as one of the guys?

SNAG: That'd be real close to homosexuality.

AAG: Exactly.

KL: Hmm-mmm.

AAG: I agree.

This is very disturbing news. So if a woman is honest and revealing and open and just absolutely herself around you –

AAG: It depends on whether she wants to be a friend. And there is a big difference between being one of the guys –

SNAG: And being a friend.

KL: The signals don't have to be completely artificial in order to say, "I don't want to be one of the guys."

Okay. Care to elaborate?

[prolonged silence]

[crescendoing nervous laughter]

SNAG: There are a lot of different roles that women can play, other than being one of the guys, where they can also be very relaxed. One of the ones we were talking about is the sister role, the confidante, the mother, you know all of those different things. And from relationships in which you're clearly defined as a woman, it's not so difficult to make that relationship to girlfriend, or lover, or something else. I mean, I have certainly had women who I've just treated as friends for a long time and who have treated me as a friend for a long time, and then there was some shift, some subtle change that took place in our relationship. I have never found myself in a relationship with a woman who was part of, like, the foosball gang or whatever. You know, the beer-chugging gang on Friday nights who then you ended up in bed with... That would be too much. But a woman that you knew and who never really... how can I say it? Never really completely squelched the sexual aspect of the relationship? If there were always just a little bit of that there, a little bit of sexual tension there I can see it going on to another type of relationship. But otherwise, I agree with these guys completely. If you have established yourself as one of the guys, forget it. You need a whole new set of guys. And they may even set you up with their friends. They'll be guffawing. "He doesn't realize what he's getting into." Not because they don't like you or think that you're worth knowing, but just the thought of one of their friends going out with you is going to seem really kind of bizarre to them.

What I find interesting is that another guy who is not present… actually, several men I know have posited the theory that there is always sexual tension present between men and women.

SNAG: Yeah, I know, I've heard that.

AAG: Yeah.

You've heard that, huh?

[prolonged silence]

AAG: Well, a woman can be one of the guys, but if she displays some flirtation, she can still retain the ability to get out of that syndrome and into –

KL: If initially you haven't lost completely the –

SNAG: If it hasn't been squelched –

AAG: It depends on the time frame. How far into it she is.

SNAG: Sure. And I've known women before where every so often the issue… you know, you'd be talking about sex or sexuality every so often, and a woman like that would say something like, "Well, you've never really had the best, have you?" or something like that. And that's as far as it goes, but that's all she needs to do to –

AAG: Plant the seed.

SNAG: "I'm still a woman."

KL: But nothing can be quite so surprising as getting that from one of the guys. At the same time, getting that message, I think –

SNAG: Once it's been firmly established –

KL: Once it's been firmly established, that kind of thing can be –

SNAG: Kind of sickening?

KL: Yeah. Or surprising, at least. I don't know quite what to do with that.

Not from what I hear.

AAG: We've got somebody in our office who's one of the guys. I mean, she talks more to the guys than to the girls, but there's always sexual innuendo in there. She's always –

SNAG: Yeah.

AAG: Teasing the guys –

SNAG: Yeah!

AAG: So that she always leaves it open so that –

SNAG: Yeah.

AAG: If she wants to go beyond being one of the guys, she can. That teasing and sexual innuendo keeps the door open.

Two of you have mentioned sexual innuendo. Is there anything else in a woman's behavior that would keep the door open?

SNAG: I think being stunningly beautiful might help.

[raucous laughter]

Thank you for your honesty.

AAG: That's true.

SNAG: Because deep down inside –

AAG: There's an attraction.

SNAG: Yeah, there was always an attraction that he never really quite let go of.

KL: That's right.

AAG: But face it: if you're around a girl that's stunningly beautiful, you feel intimidated around her. Right? I mean, I do.

KL: Of course, there's that constant awareness, though, of –

AAG: I don't see where a girl who's really stunningly beautiful could become one of the guys.

SNAG: It would be extremely difficult.

KL: It would take a lot of effort on both sides, I think.

SNAG: Also, I think women like that have a different sense of self awareness, because they see themselves as sex objects. So their whole approach to men is different.

AAG: What was that, Kathy, the "Barbie doll syndrome?"

SNAG: And I would think that even if they're not airheads. Just because you're good-looking doesn't mean you're an airhead – isn't that right, Kathy?

Good save, SNAG.

SNAG: Their whole approach to men is going to be a lot more wary, because guys are always coming on to them.

AAG: Yup.

SNAG: They're not going to have that

relaxation, that sense of "Hey, guys, what are you doing after work? What do you say we go hoist a few?"

AAG: It's a different part that somebody who's really beautiful plays. They don't have to be one of the guys. They always play the part of the tease.

KL: It's hard for them not to be aware of what they look like.

AAG: Sure.

KL: Somebody's always reminding them.

AAG: Sure.

KL: Through a stare or –

Salivating.

KL: Or salivating. Dropping things as people pass by.

AAG: Talking to a left one and then talking to a right one.

[laughter and applause]

KL: The center will not hold.

AAG: Are you going to print that?

[prolonged silence]

AAG: Okay. Have we beat that one to death?

It went somewhere I certainly didn't expect it to. My, my.

SNAG: Gee, Kathy, don't you have any other things you want to ask us?

KL: We branched off from, "What can a woman do to avoid that?" To being stunningly beautiful.

Well, then, let's back up a second. If a woman is first getting to know you, what sorts of things would she do that would subliminally signal to you, "This person is romance material"? Or, "This person would go out with you"?

SNAG: When you talk to guys, and you're getting to know guys, there's a certain superficial level that goes on. There are certain boundaries, certain things you don't talk about. You don't talk about things that are real, real deep-down important to you. Except maybe if it's somebody that you really know or you're really attracted to. That's about it. Whereas sometimes with women – I don't know about you guys, but I know with myself – with women I can unload a little bit more, a little bit sooner to them, and if they can reply to me on a confidante level, then you've established a special bond right away.

AAG: Evidently you haven't had one that's just grabbed your heart, pulled it out, thrown it on the floor, and stomped on it a few times. They'll use it against you.

SNAG: Oh, well, yeah. I guess what I'm saying is that's one way of establishing a relationship right away that says that you're not going to be a "buddy" or a guy like that. Most of the women I've known who've been one of the guys have been women at work.

AAG: Right.

SNAG: Women that I used to work with or women that I work with now. And there's already a certain hands-off thing that's in the air. Unless unmistakable signals are sent out, I'm not going to mess with them.

AAG: Most men can't talk about deep emotions. It's something that's cloaked. And really, women don't get into those deep emotions unless it's more of a bedroom atmosphere, as kind of "the afterglow," shall we say.

KL: Either that, or drunk.

SNAG: You've been at a party or something and been introduced to somebody, and started talking and asked something like, "Well, how do you like Houston?" And instead of saying, "Well, the weather's nice, you know, but I don't like my job," she'll say something like –

AAG: "I can't meet anybody."

SNAG: Or she'll say something that's kind of surprising like, "Well, my boyfriend left me and I'm wondering if I need to take some self-improvement classes, or if there's something wrong with me." That's your chance to say, "Oh, you're fine just the way you are."

AAG: Let me ask a question beyond that. What if she says, "Yeah, I'm new to town, I don't have that much to do. My husband lives in another city, and things are pretty dull around here"?

[incredulous laughter]

AAG: This is a real –

KL: Right this way, fella.

AAG: Would you really go after that? I'm asking from a…realistic standpoint.

SNAG: Gee, when I think of all the times that's happened to me, I've got to remember how I responded.

AAG: You know, what really shows me that somebody's interested in me is when a girl will sit and listen to you and ask questions about YOU! Not, "I this, this, this, and this" –

SNAG: Waiting for you to finish so she can start talking about her own perspective –

AAG: But truly asking questions. "Well, what do you like? How was your day? Tell me about what you did."

KL: It's called active listening.

AAG: Exactly. Guys love to talk.

So if she feeds your ego and it doesn't seem to be forced or phony, that's a good thing.

AAG: Exactly. Feeding ego: "Tell me about your day. Tell me about what happened here." And if a guy gets a chance to get things off of his chest and be able to talk to somebody… I think this goes back to what you were saying of being able to say things to someone that you wouldn't be able to tell other people. It's a vulnerability. "Gosh, I really had a bad day and let me tell you why." You wouldn't go telling people in the office about that necessarily, but to be able to tell somebody else that –

SNAG: That makes you special.

KL: But at the same time it puts the guy at center stage as well.

AAG: And at ease.

SNAG: On the other hand I must say I've read plenty of those things where they say the same thing about men; you know, in men's magazines they always say: "Do you listen to her? Do you ask her questions about herself? Do you really care about her day?" And they say, well: NO. Just be yourself and you'll be doing so much better than all those other guys.

It sounds like three things so far. If you find yourself unexpectedly opening up to someone, someone opens up to you, or someone takes a great interest in you, these are three things that might indicate that this person could be romantic potential, rather than "a guy," right? It also sounds like the environment has something to do with it. You meet a women in a work environment, you tend to –

SNAG: You meet a woman in a bar, assuming you meet her at all, there's going to be a lot of hackles raised immediately. One of the best ways to meet somebody is through somebody else. That's why I like parties, because there's a certain legitimacy for you being there. You've got no excuse for being in a bar on Saturday night by yourself; come on. And you could be any rapist or –

AAG: That's why all the bars do such good business on Thursday and Friday nights.

KL: At least someone thought well enough of you to invite you to a party.

AAG: At least you know this person's probably not going to come over to your house and boil a bunny rabbit.

KL: You can't rule that out until the third or fourth date.

AAG: This person doesn't have a fetish for knives.

SNAG: At least you know who to blame if she does.

At what point does her showing interest or extending an invitation suddenly become too much? One thing I've finally realized is that the best – seems to me the wisest – policy is an attitude of receptivity and letting men choose timing, and letting them issue invitations.

SNAG: They've got to know you're interested. You can carry this receptive stuff too far.

I understand that.

SNAG: A lot of guys are real shy.

AAG: True.

SNAG: Nobody wants to make a fool of themselves. Listen: this happened to me. I met a woman who was introduced to me by another friend. We were tending bar together at a charity function, and this woman spent the entire evening with me walking around and talking. And we talked about all the things that we both had in common, and all the stuff we enjoyed, and at the end of it all I said something like, "You know, I really like you. I'd like to get your number. I'd like to call you." And she said, "Oh, okay," and she gave me her number. I don't know why she did, because she refused to ever, ever go out with me after that. You know?

I know about this. Wasn't me!

SNAG: I thought you'd get a kick out of it.

Thank you.

SNAG: But no, I mean, you'd want to know that a woman's interested, and if she's not, you don't want to waste your time, either. The older we get, the more gun-shy we get.

Well, this is fascinating.

The question was: What would a woman do in your first couple of weeks of getting to know her that would indicate that she's romance potential? Dating potential?

AAG: Slight physical contact.

SNAG: Hiking her skirts whenever you're around.

Besides physical contact, how about prolonged eye contact?

AAG: Eye contact says a lot.

SNAG: It says a lot, yeah. You don't want to be corny about it. You don't want to swoon.

KL: Or play blinking contests.

AAG: Well, it goes back to what I was saying about if the girl asks the guy a lot of questions: "Tell me about your day." Then she can give you that prolonged eye contact. That's flirting. It's more of a, "Tell me about yourself." Boy, does that open it up. All she has to do is just sit back and stare at him or watch his eyes and that's a flirtatious activity.

KL: Also, all of my jokes seem to be a lot funnier than they are to ordinary civilians.

SNAG: I'd keep the physical stuff down to a minimum. That can scare people off.

I'm not saying things to do. I'm saying: What signals, what – to you – says, "Aahh, this person's interested."

AAG: How about something like this: A guy grabbing a girl like that on the shoulder, or touching… nothing wrong with that, but that opens it up right there. Or vice versa.

KL: That opens up ambiguity.

AAG: Or a girl grabbing a guy, kind of on the shoulder or every once in a while putting the hand on the arm –

SNAG: But again, I'd keep that stuff down to a minimum. You really are sort of violating space. And you can send out too strong of a signal.

AAG: You can overdo that.

SNAG: You really can overdo that. I think you're right: I think eye contact. I can usually tell if a woman's interested real quick just by eye contact. And then I'll be surprised if it turns out a woman's interested and there hasn't been any eye contact.

AAG: Are we on page 10 of the *Compendium* now?

I think so! Any final non sequiturs anyone cares to throw out?

AAG: I knew a female attorney that was sort of one of the guys.

KL: Tell us the story. Please!

AAG: And she could sit and talk. She loved sports; her dad brought her up as sort of a tomboy. She was gorgeous. She was a blonde, blue-eyed Joyce Davenport[15] from *Hill Street Blues*. She could talk to guys just like

[15] For those of you following along at home: not me. Definitely not me.

any of the other guys, but I tell you: she was a real vamp. People fell over her. She was beautiful; she was very intelligent. But most of the time she asked more questions about the person. Again, more, "Tell me about your day; tell me about this." She could drink like the rest of the guys. I tell you, you just hoped she would say something like –

SNAG: Jesus, where do I meet this girl?

KL: Yeah, I was going to ask.

AAG: Well, she's married now. She's one of those that we said that she had seasonal boyfriends. She would date a guy for three months and get rid of him; pick up a new one, date him three months. And there was an actual fan club, as we called it, really, an alumni club that used to meet, of all of her exes. And eventually she went through most of the men around her and got married to somebody in another city.

SNAG: That makes sense.

KL: Yeah, it does.

AAG: Her reputation got around. Fantastic in bed, but people soon learned about what her modus operandi was: date a guy for three months, squeeze out of him what she wanted to and then go on to the next one. It's funny; she would –

KL: Leaving a dry husk behind.

AAG: She would usually drop guys right after Christmas, right after her birthday in May, right after holidays.

KL: Oooooooo.

AAG: You've got the idea?

KL: It'd be a little less suspicious before, wouldn't it?

AAG: She was one that if you went out for dinner on a Saturday night and dinner was less than $60, she wouldn't consider spending the night with you. But if you spent over $60 with her, she would consider spending the night with you. Very expensive girl.

KL: This was empirically worked out over a number of different-seasoned guys.

AAG: And once the alumni association was established, a lot of these things came out. It was every month, every two months. We had this room set aside at a bar that most everybody went to. The alumni association would get in there, and we'd just… "She did this, and this. Oh, yeah, when she was in bed, would she bite you on the neck, too?" That type of thing. We always thought that some time we were going to invite her to an alumni association meeting –

SNAG: As a guest speaker –

AAG: And watch her walk in and go, "Oh! I know you, you, you, you, you, you, you, you."

KL: "What do all these people have in common? Me!"

AAG: But she was one of the guys! But she was also a vamp.

SNAG: So let this be a warning: If you do this to men, you will get talked about.

AAG: You will have alumni associations.

Thank you, thank you, guys.

What's this? Why, it looks like we have a flit-in…

ASK A GAY: Being usually unwilling to intrude, I could not help but interject. My explanation of just about all straight male behavior is that fundamentally, straight men are bored and have far too much time (and very little else) on their hands.

Those Wedding Bell Blues

T alk about a welcoming (read: inclusive) congregation. At the reception for a solstice-tide wedding at Houston's First Unitarian Universalist Church, the bride – a *Compendium* subscriber, by the way – opened the garter-flinging ritual to anyone looking for a relationship with a woman. Her announcement elicited loud responses from two members of the catering staff. The realization that he was standing directly in the line of fire triggered shrieks of disbelief from an exotically beautiful black man, whose frilly apron and floating manner of ambulation brought to mind the butler in *La Cage aux Folles* (except this server was wearing shoes). He moved, but his coworker – a petite woman in a bolero jacket and bun-hugging tuxedo pants – jumped enthusiastically into the fray. These days being what they are, she was the one who caught the prize, which she proudly brandished, for the rest of the event, on an upper arm.

When bouquet-tossing time came around, he of the apron sashayed expectantly into the throng of women. "Here's the protocol," I instructed him. "No pushing." He went home empty-handed; the bouquet flew, suspiciously directly, into the clutches of the bride's older sister. (The tosser has since explained that this outcome was unintentional; her preferred targets were at opposite sides of the mob, and her throwing arm subconsciously split the difference by lobbing the flowers down the middle.)

"It was a set-up," an on-looker said to me in consolation, which was ludicrous in light of my well-documented attitude towards this ritual. (I once backed so far out of the line of fire that I left a hotel lobby and watched from behind the safety of a glass door; the last time I took part, every woman kept her arms at her side while the bouquet splattered apart on the floor.) "It usually is," I answered. The only time I've caught one, the bride walked up to me and tossed it at my stomach. (In 1979, in case anyone's curious, and no doubt someone is.)

The preceding ceremony, by the way, surpassed the reception in inclusivity, invoking just about every imaginable benevolent deity except the usual. Walking meditation-style to Wagner's "Pilgrim's Chorus,"[16] the groomsmen brought an array of offerings to the altar that included – yes indeed! – a bunch of bananas and a huge, long loaf of bread. Continuing the theme of not denying a vital element of what's really going on here, the matron of honor read an extensive, slightly sanitized passage from a steamy Sumerian poem about the goddess Inanna welcoming her consort Damuzi to her, uh, temple. As the speaker launched into Inanna's crescendoing queries, cryptic smiles spread among those of us who'd been party to the bride's own impassioned readings of this work. "Who will plow my body?" may have been what the congregation heard, but the grammatical object that resounded in our memories was "vulva."

---

[16] I want to make it clear once and for all that, as much as he seems to have permeated my universe, this is not my favorite composer. I'm not the one with the Wagner fixation; Doc is, and I would caution any of you from getting to know this man too well, lest you, too, be infected with this pernicious disease.

Till ? Do Us Part

In which class goes out the window

M ost of the groom's family boycotted the ceremony. One of the groomsmen drank a half a bottle of Jack Daniel's before arriving at the church. The groomsmen wore tuxes with stripes alternating shiny and dull black, and white vests embossed with shiny white paisleys. Their groomsmen's gifts – an engraved water set (a fancy beaker with a water glass) – elicited sporadic cracks about urine tests. When a pal tried to photograph them before the ceremony, Jack Daniel's friend – who is a 6'10" ex-college-athlete – threatened to rip the shutterbug's arm out of its socket.

The minister traveled to the altar by wheelchair; the wedding party lifted both passenger and transport into officiating position. The chapel was lit only by candlelight, some of which emanated from hurricane lamps being carried by the bridesmaids. Holding glowing flames below chin level created a gruesome, Halloween-monster effect on their faces, similar to that of pointing a flashlight up at your chin. The most pronounced impact was on the bride's sister, who, without benefit of lighting, already resembled the psychic in *Poltergeist*.

Despite the subdued lighting, four camcorders (two in the balcony) and a still camera captured every should-have-been sacred moment.

Before the bride began her processional, the organ broke into "Summertime." (The calendar said: November.) The congregation remained standing, after the bride arrived (carrying a predominantly plastic bouquet), for some 15 to 20 minutes; the minister showed no awareness of a problem with people standing, since he was sitting. Before the vows were exchanged, the minister announced that the groom had selected some music to honor the bride. A man played the guitar and sang The Troggs' "Love Is All Around." ("I feel it in my fingers, I feel it in my toes...") The guitarist saved the day – and the congregation's feet – when the bridal consultant dispatched him from the back of the church to whisper a message to the bride's mother. She sat down. Then everyone else did.

During the vows, the bride[17] whined a specially prepared speech promising obedience and subjugation. It was noticeable to the audience that she was whispering portions of the speech to herself before speaking them out loud, because she had forgotten what she was going to say. Ensconced in a pew, the wife of the aforesaid Jack-Daniel's-charged groomsman lost her composure so badly that she bent over to avoid drawing attention to her stifled hysterical laughter. Her situation only worsened when her male companion (and our informant) put his arm around her and said, consolingly, "There, there, I know you always get emotional at times like this."

The pious words being intoned at the altar bore little relationship to the personality that everyone had been putting up with. In the days before the wedding, the bride had spent a lot of time pointing her finger at people (especially her fiancé), and nastily berating guests – some of whom had gone to great expense and bother to arrange time off work and to travel

---

[17] Who had instituted the revolutionary practice of one member of the bridal couple hosting a shower for the other by throwing a Craftsman tool shower for her hubby-to-be. (The goal, which she achieved, was preventing a bachelor's party. Her intent was to have all his friends under one roof – hers – and take their keys away from them as they arrived.) She invited 50 people. Five showed up.

from several states away to attend the Friday ceremony (timed for the sole convenience of the couple, who wanted to start their honeymoon by accepting a solicitation for a free, Saturdays-only look at a beach timeshare condo) – about their choice of wedding present.[18,19] At the rehearsal dinner the night before, her family greatly outnumbered his (even though his, per tradition, was footing the bill), due to his family's objections to his choice of bride, and her having invited as many relatives as she could think of.

After the ceremony, the assembly adjourned to a fellowship hall in the Baptist church for the music-and-alcohol-free reception. Getting out of the chapel took a while, however, because the exit was blocked by the reception line, which was set up in the foyer.

Several of the groom's friends detoured through the parking lot, where they'd had the foresight to stash a cooler of beer and a supply of Certs. To amuse themselves, they went back and forth between the car and the party (where they threatened to spike the punch). A problem with this coping mechanism (besides triggering the recurring observation, "Man, all of you smell like Certs!") was the absence in the fellowship hall of a men's restroom – a circumstance that only increased the necessity and frequency of trips out to the car.

In the hall, photographs of the bride and groom at different stages of growing up surrounded their respective cakes. The bride's wedding portrait (enlarged to several feet tall) stood on an easel adjacent to her table. A

---

[18] And now for some equal-opportunity disparaging: when this particular groom was the best man for the groomsman who keeps being singled out in this story, he could not be bothered to take time off work (a night shift) for the bachelor's party and left the rehearsal dinner early.

[19] More of their gifts came from Home Depot than from department stores. The couple had in fact registered with Home Depot. We are not making this up. Not any of it.

basket chock full of miniatures of the same photo had been carefully placed by the sign-in book. Two of the guests were startled by the appearance of the groom's cake, which had been baked and decorated to replicate a boat that they, the guests, own, with figures of a groom carrying his bride in flagrant trespass over the threshold onto the boat. Already confused, one of the owners misread the name iced across the craft as *S.S. Minnow* and wandered about the reception serenading people, "for a three hour tour."

The bride and groom lingered so long in the church having photos taken that by the time they sashayed into the reception, most of the food and the guests were gone.

Before the party's end, the toasty group set up a pool of bets on how long this marriage will last. The oft-aforementioned groomsman is holding the money while the clock runs.

Fool's Paradise

Morris Dancing and Moos

April 1. Leave town for a change of scenery and a wedding. The destination is a meadow outside Austin. It's home to a co-op of mystic Catholics (one of whom is the bride, and most of whom have built houses on the land), a horse, some cows, and a pair of free-range llamas that will remain visible during the entire proceedings. The two-footed witness contingent is heavily weighted towards the traditional music communities of Houston and Austin, altogether too many people who know far too much about each other. Both of Houston's squads (more correctly, "sides") of Morris Dancers[20] are present in full regalia. I propose setting up a betting pool on how many of the groom's exes will show up. Everyone laughs and looks about cautiously. Unfortunately, no one ponies up. John-the-Not-so-Terminally-Weird and I are sure at least three will surface, and exactly that many do.

We sit in folding chairs arranged in concentric circles atop a gently

---

[20] Devotees of British fertility dances that involve wearing white clothing, colored ribbons across the chest, straw hats festooned with flowers (for each virgin plucked), and jingle bells strapped to the calves, and leaping about waving white handkerchiefs or wielding large, long sticks. The term "Fool" applies, at least technically, to only one position, usually designating the side's best dancer. Traditionalists restrict this frolicsome activity to men (women, so I'm told, have their own flavor of fertile footwork), while progressives allow the genders to share this pastime. The Men of Houston embrace the first approach; Shambles takes the latter.

sloping hill. The groom joins Shambles (one of the Morris sides) in a rousing stick dance, then disappears behind a cluster of trees while his colleagues engage in a song and dance about what fools he and his bride are being. When he emerges, Shambles and the Men of Houston form an archway with their sticks for his procession. He has overlaid his dress whites with a purple paisley ankle-length toga; a wreath has appeared on his head. He moves to ground zero and sings "The Lord of the Dance," including the verse containing the line, "and they laid me on the cross," as his bride approaches, accompanied by her three prepubescent children. She is wearing a wreath and a long gown made of the same purple paisley material.

The minister praises the singing and dancing and asks for the vows. The groom sighs audibly, repeatedly. The woman in front of me, who has sung in a band with me and the groom, gets up and moves out of eye and earshot, for which I will thank her profusely at the end of the ceremony.

"As sure as my name is [x], I choose you, [y], to be my life partner," he begins. Her version is much the same, minus the stage sighs, only her laundry list of what she chooses him as kicks off with "sweetheart." The exchanging ring vows are more fervent, comparing the intertwining of the rings' metals with that of their souls, so different and yet unified in a common purpose.

A cow moos. "Editorial comment," says the Men of Houston's Fool.

After the groom makes vows and hands a token confirming the same to each of the children, the minister proclaims them husband and wife, "by the authority granted me by...the entire universe!" The family holds hands and sings, "The Lobster Quadrille," which sets Lewis Carroll's verses to a traditional British melody. I fix my gaze on the oldest child, a nine-year-old boy, and wonder how long it will take for him to realize how far outside the norm, even for outside the norm, this ceremony has flown. The family ambles out of the circle; the Morris Dancers, hankies waving, jump into the fray; the guests stand up and disperse. I thank the woman who moved out of my line of sight. "We were very well-behaved," I say. "We were very well-behaved," she says. We repeat the sentence as the entirety of our commentary on the ceremony, to all who ask.

The reception is at a dance hall on private land inside a state park, a location as out of the way and hard to reach as the wedding site. On the way, swift braking reflexes narrowly prevent John and me from becoming one with the bumper and trunk of the preceding car, when an enormous flock of low-flying geese spellbind driver and passenger. Inside the hall, someone has hung a poster board with the schedule of activities written in Magic Marker. The list begins "The Sorting of the Line," appended by a couple of names, one of which is disconcertingly familiar from law school days, and ends, "The Presentation of the Strawberries," in between are sets of songs for contradancing and singing.

Outside, under the pines, the contradancers and singers reveal a basic dissonance in life philosophy immediately after dinner. The first faction and those friendly to it cooperate when a man[21] and a woman bark out instructions to form two lines, then rearrange themselves according to a series of seemingly irrelevant criteria, such as birthdays and number of years married. The rest of us move out of earshot, behind the building, to nurture emerging bad attitudes and sing British folk songs in multi-part

---

[21] …who turns out to be exactly the person I'd suspected from list on the poster board – a lawyer who'd stayed on, after graduation, as a resident in the University of Texas' German Haus co-op, which he showed me around when I briefly (a length of time that expired before the end of my tour) considered moving in – I recall we sat on the roof at one point during his pitch – and who stands out in my memory as the folk dancer who set himself apart most dramatically from the legions of guys who dated my friend Nancy by wrapping a dinner salad in a large lettuce leaf and eating it like a taco.

harmony.

The lines, once properly sorted in every unimaginable way, file back into the hall and leave us to our grumbling, but not before someone recommends bombing the building to prevent the menace of contradancing. When the songs turn too religious and the smokers too incessantly to their cigarettes, I decide to form my own judgment about the activity indoors. Contradancing is a line-dance cousin to square dancing, but far more prolonged and complicated than anything grade school phys. ed. classes ever put me through.[22] Making it through one dance leaves me questioning the deservability of its reputation as reprehensible, but also disinclined to pursue further research, at least at the moment. John voices the desire to ask the groom to be his partner for the next dance. When he later confesses this to the bride, she says he should have. Instead, he kisses the groom on the lips. The dancing switches to two-stepping and waltzing. The bride takes a seat on the sidelines and breast-feeds her two-year-old daughter.

During my only unchaperoned conversation with her, I grapple for a topic guaranteed not to offend. The weather! How lucky they are that the skies have been so clear and blue and the temperature so lovely. "Yes," she gushes, "It's a love vortex."

---

[22] Which introduced third-graders to such noble themes as "Mademoiselle from Armentiers (inky dinky parlez-vous)" and, my favorite even at such a tender age, "Pistol Packin' Mama."

The Equal-Opportunity Employer

*What looks at first glance like dry land is often smack in the midst of the
Straits of Confusion on the High Seas of Androgyny and Ambiguity.*

When I moved into my current office building, the tenant across the
hall was a travel agency that specialized in European hotel bookings. The
owner, Peter, was one of those men who look to have been born with upper
class elegance; a characteristic he accentuated with such props as finely
tailored sports jackets, a Jaguar, and a convincing British accent.[23]

He didn't know it, but his days in the building were numbered; the new
owner, who was my lure into this situation, had already privately staked
out the agency's space for his firm's next home. It turned out there were
some things we didn't know about Peter as well.

I hadn't been there but a couple of weeks when the first hint surfaced,
so forcefully that it got the attention of everyone in the building. All I
noticed was louder than usual shouting erupting from his office. When
things quieted down, I passed his secretary in the hall. She was shaking
her head and desperate for an audience. "Didn't you see the police?" she
demanded. Noooooo. Somehow this had escaped my notice. She filled in
the picture. Peter had fired a female assistant that morning. She'd taken the
news about as lamely as he'd conveyed it. He ordered her off the premises;
she refused to leave. He called the police and, in the meantime, pushed

[23] Which is not, as we know, proof of nationality, or even of historic residence.
Matter of fact, my impression, based on his last name, his handwriting, and the
city of origin of the posters in his office, was that he was German.

their argument into a more physical realm. The incident did rid his office of this employee, who finally exited under police escort, but it also left his secretary disposed to spilling his sordid details to a stranger.

What sourcebook does this labor skirmish sound like? (I wonder, wonder…) The employee of another tenant confirmed the obvious suspicion. Just a week earlier, she'd investigated unlikely noises in the kitchen, which is directly opposite the door to her office. What she saw was Peter and his doomed assistant groping, playing kissy-face, and otherwise engaging in behavior that shed the light of clarity on the woman's later refusal to leave.

A week or two after the police escort, Peter's office again became the point of origin for another bout of shouting. This one was loud enough that the substance could be detected. (Hell, it couldn't be avoided.) Someone was attempting to collect a debt, and someone was quite successfully avoiding it. The second voice was familiar enough; the first belonged to a young Frenchman, who'd been in the building before, and who we gossipmongers later learned was the representative of a family-owned chain of hotels that claimed to be owed tens of thousands of dollars.

Once again the police were summoned. Once again someone who dared confront Peter left in the company of men in blue. Once again Peter's secretary mouthed off about him as she walked up and down the hall (this time exclaiming how glad she was to have given notice of leaving). And once again, the woman whose door looks into the kitchen supplied a most intriguing puzzle piece. In an earlier investigative peek, she'd seen Peter pinching the young Frenchman's ass.

Soon enough Peter gave notice and moved. I don't know anyone in the building who bothered to say goodbye.

Another Fool Moon...

...another scud lust missile detonating in public.

The latest was not so much omnidirectional as successful. This one went off at a party in a driveway that had been filled with furniture to simulate a cozy den.[24] The set-up consisted of a long, cushy couch, a deep, cushy chair, and a beat-up love seat, arranged in a U-shape, end tables with working lamps, a central coffee table, and semi-circles of folding chairs behind the love seat. The arrangement facilitated communal intimacy in ways that our host had not foreseen.

The missile started out, as they always do, looking like just another party guest – in this case, a woman we'll call Tracy. She arrived in the company of a man whom she left in the confines of the host's garage apartment (the dimensions of which had inspired throwing parties in the driveway), while she settled in on the long, cushy couch outside. She nuzzled up to the nearest body, which belonged to a man we'll call Luke. With people sitting and talking all around – including on the Luke-free side of the couch – she got her target in a prolonged liplock that included obvious deep mouth excavation. Then she returned to nuzzling, eyes shut as if in sleep, or reverie, or a substance-induced stupor.

When a female guest stood at the back of the couch to talk to a friend

---

[24] The very same driveway that was invaded by a truckload of drunken, sword-waving Pasadenans, including the orthodontically-enhanced, scantily clad young woman who earned the moniker "Hi-my-name-is-Rachel" from "How Can You Tell It's Performance Art?" on p. 171.

across the driveway, Tracy languidly lifted an arm and reached for the woman's breasts, a development that led to (a) her hand being swatted off, (b) the male guests voicing the consensus that they'd like to see a woman's hands on another woman's breast, (c) a female guest leaping onto a succession of men and pinching their nipples, and (d), ultimately, the granting of the men's wish in a way that utilized none of Tracy's body parts. Still in whatever state was keeping her eyes closed, Tracy took no notice.

She didn't react either when a man ran into the driveway and yelled at her that he would find his way home and she didn't have to worry about him being around for the rest of the weekend because he would find someplace else to stay. (Scuttlebutt later identified him as an out-of-town boyfriend.) Wide-spread gawking ensued. She gave him time to speed away before flinging herself, eyes still closed, across Luke's lap. A few moments later, she lurched into a full straddle, her eyes still closed. The gawking intensified. Finally taking the initiative, Luke got her to stand up and they walked away.

One of the witnesses followed. He rushed back with the news that Luke and Tracy had moved their groping to a bench around the corner. A delegation formed and marched off to inspect the proceedings. One of the inspectors soon presented an eyewitness report. The pair had left the bench for a parked car, in the comparative privacy of which Tracy was ministering to Luke's growing needs. Our informant ran up to the car and asked what was going on, at which point Luke turned the ignition and took off.

The morning's paper screamed news of Princess Diana's death and of an 18-wheeler catching fire and tumbling from an elevated highway not two miles from the driveway. What a fool moon, indeed.

The Strai(gh)ts of Confusion

And now, the tale of a candidate for High Seas poster child who capsized in its turbulent currents. This played out a couple of years ago, when I was still renting office space in inner city Houston from an attorney.[25] The office was reeling from a summer of secretary roulette (a karmic penalty, on an installment payment plan, being extracted by the gods for the office manager's persistent, inscrutable staff mishandling) when he – let's call him Will – hired someone without first introducing the candidate around the office. Notified of this occurrence, I trundled downstairs and stopped dead in my tracks at the sight of the newcomer. A few years earlier, Will had refused even to interview an applicant with good experience and an eagerness to work for insulting wages, just because of the conclusions that might be drawn from a male attorney having a male secretary in a predominantly gay neighborhood. And now, perched beside him at the receptionist's desk was a pretty boy, immaculate in grooming and diction, with the starkest steel rod jammed up his spine.

---

[25] We hope we've sat on this next item long enough for the culprit to move far out of orbit (not to mention earshot); The one who didn't understand why everyone else in the office got upset when he hired his barely-English-speaking daughter-in-law (who had first come to the West only six weeks earlier for her wedding) to answer the phones; Who didn't understand why I got upset when I couldn't get into the office because he'd changed the front door lock without telling me (though he had, he pointed out, left a key in my mail tray, behind the locked door...). Who didn't understand why I was moving.

"This is William," Will said,[26] hastening to add that William had recently married, and he and his wife were expecting.

Uh-huh, I thought.

I didn't have any problem with the flavor of this new presence. I've always fancied having a male secretary. And besides, William was competent. And motivated. And ambitious. And outgoing. And capable of writing down a phone number without mangling the digits. What's more, he demonstrated allegiance to my motto, "Keep 'em guessing!" His wife (whose gender was quickly verified as female) called him several times daily. He seemed genuinely fond of her. And she really was pregnant; in fact, the condition was so precarious, due to some pre-existing health problems, that he wore a beeper just so she could reach him if an emergency arose (which did, several times, endangering the lives of both mother and child). Okay. Maybe my gaydar had blared in vain.

Then again, maybe not. A gay friend who dropped in for lunch swore William was cruising him; even I saw the 180-degree neck swivel in my friend's direction as William's Camaro roared out of the driveway. Then there was the ongoing fact that William got along extraordinarily well with me. But that wasn't necessarily determinative. Plenty of secretaries have been favorably disposed to me.[27] Plenty of secretaries have walked into my office and announced a need to talk to me. A few have even prefaced their outpouring with a heart-felt, "Please don't tell Will this!" But only one, so far, has capped this sequence of events by closing the door

---

[26] Any armchair psychologists out there care to comment on the fact that the only men that Will ever invited into our midst, either as tenant or employee, bore his first name?

[27] Maybe it's got something to do with the fact that unlike so many in my profession, I treat them as the human beings that they are.

and coming out.

This confession was not a recognition of my blood curse; It was a preemptive strike. William'd been fielding messages for me from members of the Gay Men's Chorus, and he was sure that one of them would recognize him and blow his cover. Apparently, he'd had quite the notorious

reputation in his younger days. Once he unloaded this secret, William decided to keep the information flowing. He volunteered the information – I wasn't going to ask – that he really was the father of the child his wife was carrying and that his orientation was – I really wasn't going to ask – quadrasexual.[28]

He was always talking up various schemes for businesses he wanted to launch, and when I was around he'd elaborate on the gay slant to the moment's dream. He'd self-published a book (under a different last name) about the bar lifestyle, which he insisted on lending me in the hopes that I could help him find a marketing consultant. An editor would have been a better first step.[29] I kept mum about either role. Native hucksterism steered him soon enough to a way to promote the book himself: selling it at a fundraiser for an AIDS relief organization and donating a portion of the sales to the non-profit. When one actually agreed to go along for the ride, William escalated the event into an evening of nationally-known stand-up comics. As one after another phoned to accept the invitation to perform,

[28] You looked; you asked for it: men, women, children, and animals.

[29] Maybe it comes from growing up in a tight-assed WASP neighborhood, but I prefer my tasteless humor to be a little less coarse and a little more grammatically correct.

William reacted recklessly, hooting with glee in the reception area within earshot of his employer, who abandoned characteristic nosiness when the fundraiser's beneficiary was identified.

It was during William's tenure that I fled the building. William was the only coworker who asked me to lunch on my last day. We shared a beer and traded stories of how weird life can be, and he offered to provide after-hours support services for me in my new office. He made good on his word. Besides calling now and again to swap bad jokes, he stopped by my office to help out several times on the way home. The last time I saw him, he refused to take payment because he believed that providing notary services was part of being in the legal profession.

Several months later, Will's part-time college student worker phoned in a panic. She'd just learned William wouldn't be coming in – not just that day, but probably ever again. His wife had called with the news that he'd tried to commit suicide and left the state the night before to check into a hospital for alcoholism. I got linked into this phone tree out of desperation; the student was alone in the office and didn't know how to reach her employer, who'd gone out of town for the week without leaving a phone number. I gave her some leads on tracking him down. Before setting off on the chase, she gave instance after instance of William's drinking of late affecting his work. I hadn't seen anything, except that one drink at lunch.

Will's response to this turn of events was irritation. When he got back, he phoned me to tell me exactly this. And to apologize. I was amazed by the verb, but even more so by the object. He apologized for all the problems William had caused me when I was a tenant. Not for my having been summoned for help by the staff he'd abandoned. Not for his previous employees' telling callers that I was out when I wasn't. Not for his own hand dropping into the mail a settlement check that'd been delivered to me. But for something that never, ever occurred.

With that, the information flow on William ceased. On the latest map of the High Seas of Androgyny & Ambiguity, Will is marooned at Cape Clueless, with no hope of rescue, while the felled, valiant sailor of this tale remains MIA. May he have found firm footing on dry land, far from those sanity-churning Straits of Confusion.

Walk on the Weird Side

Just Say No to H₂O

Recent medical evidence suggests a friend has mutated into an alien being.

Granted, there are those among my acquaintances who may actually *be* alien beings. They certainly act like it. A few even claim off-planet origins, in fact (and, if you knew them, you might well concede that they have a point).

But not the person who received this scientific revelation. He's a salt-of-the-earth type, a responsible person who looks not only comfortable, but somehow *right* in a business suit, the slave of personal habits so conservative that he frequently and enthusiastically devotes entire evenings to paying bills. The only substance he regularly abuses is snack food, except during lulls of his periodic resolve to quit smoking. No question that he would define the bottom of any ranking of candidates for space cadet. But not, apparently, space invader.

It's not his idea, of course; it's simply not in the universe of thoughts that would ever cross his mind. Being a Capricorn, he does have an uncommon devotion to *terra firma* and all matters connected with it. (Although – perhaps this was the first hint of his mutation, missed by all – his inner circle is veritably crammed with Aquarians; so many that he jokes about writing a book about their care and feeding. So many that their combined force field may have affected his own structural integrity.)

No, the idea had to come from outside of him, from someone in a position of apparent authority. Quite appropriately, it came during what should have been a routine and casual incident to changing jobs: the physical. You'd think someone so innately attuned to material would have navigated that detail with flying colors. But the world is changing and so, it seems, is my friend.

An extraterrestrial lineage was not exactly what the nurse had in mind when, after the initial lab results, she called him to come back. "Everything's fine," she said offhandedly. "Your urine's just … thin." Ever respectful of processes that will ultimately lead to depositing a paycheck, he provided a second sample and awaited word that he could change his morning driving route.

The next phone call was disquieting. Its source was not personnel, but the clinic, this time announcing that the staff doctor wanted to counsel him. A minor chord sounded on a Hammond organ off in the cosmos.

The earliest appointment was four days away, four days that he spent thinking the words "witch hunt" and agonizing over what might possibly have been found in his body fluids. The problem, it turned out, was not what was in them, but what wasn't.

The sample he provided did not contain the minimal level of body salts necessary to constitute urine. That's one of the two goals of testing, the doctor admitted: to screen for drugs and to confirm that the subject of the test is in fact urine. Since it failed to meet statistical norms, what my friend's kidneys excrete isn't urine.

Now, the doctor did not imply that my friend had adulterated the specimens. For one thing, no diluents were at hand in the clinic test room (in which the faucets were shut off and deep blue water filled the toilet). For another, this person would be constitutionally unable to perform such an unethical, dishonest act, at least not without turning himself in immediately afterward.

But the doctor did not explore whether personal habits might have affected the sample. Interestingly, the ingestion of drugs was never brought up, but the amount of water my friend drinks was of particular interest.

His answer could not possibly have accounted for a substandard quality severe enough to warrant private counseling – that is, not if the being we're dealing with is human. My friend confessed to six or seven glasses daily, which approaches the eight that moms, doctors, and *Prevention* magazine have been saying for years are necessary for optimal health. The doctor coaxed out of him the admission that, yes, he had drunk some water the night before the tests; he keeps a glass at bedside and will even get up and refill it if it empties during the night.

(This last bit comes to me second-hand; I am not the Aquarian who's actually witnessed the nocturnal aquatic habits of such apparent interest to the medical profession. But the conversation between my friend and the doctor has actually resonated against my own eardrums, thanks to a highly sensitive cassette recorder that picks up surprisingly well through a jacket pocket. My friend, you see, sensed that monumental news was on the way and took pains not to miss a word of it.)

This disclosure was not what the doctor was expecting or wanting to hear. How to reconcile perfectly healthful behavior patterns with test results that refuse to comply with statistical norms?

The doctor sent the strong nonverbal signal that anyone with urine that weak is clearly un-American, at the very least. But he stopped short of breaking the obvious conclusion outright. Of course. News of such mind-

boggling magnitude must be approached cautiously and delicately.

And that must be the reason the doctor required yet a third urine test. Since this chain of events took place in the country that birthed the concept of innocent until proven guilty, it couldn't *possibly* be that this employer considers all new workers dope fiends until conclusively vindicated up to three times by their bodily emissions.

There's only one other conclusion, and it's easy to see why anyone in the medical profession would hesitate to voice it directly. My friend has crossed the line between human being and new life form. It's indisputable that he started out as an earthling. Obviously at some point he mutated into something else, or an alien entity took over his body. That would make my friend a walk-in.

Or rather, a whiz-in.

The Wag-Log

More than you want to know about a beat-up, battered bust of a dead composer, which has traveled more in a few years than most people do in a lifetime.

Houston or Bust

It's not often that the greatest composer of all time comes to town. Not in person, of course – he's been dead for more than 100 years – but by proxy in the form of a porcelain bust bearing the ill effects of a dive into the Rio Grande (and a couple of other tumbles), and the patch-up jobs that resulted.

If this smacks of a protracted prank or, even worse, something akin to performance art, well, your instincts aren't too far off.

The composer in question is Richard Wagner, whose musical genius and boundless ego convinced King Ludwig II of Bavaria to underwrite his lavish and lengthy (some might say interminable) operas of Germanic myths. His bust is about a foot tall, with visibly glued fracture lines, gaps at the neck, and a triangular hole in his forehead. The battered creation's couriers were two college-educated (chronological) adults who devoted almost five days to the project. One was Wagner's caretaker, Doc (his preferred of several pseudonyms). I was the other. And no, nobody twisted our arms.

The original hook for the visit was a "Bring your favorite statue to meet Wagner" event at the Orange Show, Houston's center for folk art weirdness. Our purpose mushroomed into carting the bust through Houston's rampant oddness and videotaping it and, we hoped, bystanders' reactions. The real thrust turned out to be an insidious and pervasive stupidity that spiraled out from the crossing of our paths.

Unlike me, Doc was not a newcomer to sticking an inanimate object in front of a camera lens. He uses the bust (which he bought in a Salvation Army store for six bits and usually keeps at home in Tempe, Arizona, alongside bowling trophies) as the focus of travel photographs. These he compiles into photo-essay travelogues with commentary from Wagner's point of view.

How he got started is a convoluted story, having to do with a devotion to the maestro's music dating back to childhood and trading mail art with an Ohio couple who published photos of a bowling pin in various locales. Doc's first Wagner effort sealed my fate as a rabid fan and enthusiastic pen pal.

Over the years, Doc had sent the occasional cryptic communication to the *Ladies' Fetish & Taboo Compendium of Urban Anthropology* – a quarterly newsletter-cum-diary that I publish, edit, and, for the most part, write. It wasn't till *Wagner's Hollywood* arrived that his mail stood out from the barrage of largely incoherent weirdness that pours into my post office box that I bothered to write back.

Wagner's Albuquerque quickly followed, bearing a jacket blurb cribbed from my letter and accompanying an inscribed photo of the bust in a Travelodge shower, with instructions to "cherish it forever and ever, world without end, amen." By the time *Wagner's Mysterious San Diego* appeared (dedicated to my zine editrix persona), our letters were already contemplating a joint inspection of my city.

I had in mind a variation on the Orange Show Eyeopeners tours – amazing backdrops such as the Beer Can House, Cleveland Turner's fabulous plant-covered house, Pigdom, eyesore sculptures, a valve from the *Hindenburg*, interactive architecture at Rice University, and the like. "Sounds like Wagner fodder," Doc wrote in an early letter.

A newspaper calendar editor fell into hysterics over the Orange Show's press release; both dailies and alternative weeklies published notices of the event. Friends heard public service announcements on KUHF, the local NPR affiliate, which in mentioning the name of my zine actually put the word "fetish" on the classical airwaves.

After I got the first PSA report, I immediately rang up the announcer and personally invited him to join the festivities at the Orange Show. Responding with admirable diplomacy and courtesy, he did not discourage my offer to bring Wagner by the station ("We're open 24 hours a day and our listeners are free to bring a bust of Wagner to the station any time they want to"), and later sealed his own fate as Wagner-visitee by using this event as the topic for shift-changing banter with another program announcer who just so happened to be a subscriber to my zine, albeit not voluntarily. When the entourage descended upon the station, the latter program host refused to come out of the production room, but the former, as well as the program director, we'll have you know, quite graciously greeted the greatest composer of all time. Who says classical music lovers need be stodgy?

My formal introduction to the guest of honor took place in the front seat of my car in the airport parking lot. Wagner appeared surprisingly detached: his head had come off during the flight. One of Doc's first acts on Gulf Coast soil was to serve as a human vise for his just-glued companion.

The mishap signaled the ridiculous waters we would constantly tread. The technological advance from still camera to video was itself no great leap in the Wagner chronicles – as if to keep us from taking either our project or abilities too seriously, our borrowed camcorder was missing its instruction booklet. We never figured out how to do anything but record.

The tour, which redefined the concept of whirlwind, began within an hour of their deplaning. The first stop was the Beer Can House, the Milkovisch home at 222 Malone. Doc tasted Houston weirdness, and I glimpsed the way of Wagner – the unexpected spectacle of a tall, slender, ponytailed man holding a bust at arm's length with one hand while positioning an Instamatic with the other. "How did you think I did this?" he asked, assuring me that I'd get used to it.

At the door of Sonora del Norte, a restaurant across from the convention center (point of interest: a Texas shaped arrangement of cattle skulls and wall of pickup truck beds), we shared hesitations about the propriety of videotaping inside. We then walked into a dining room dominated by a birthday celebration for a woman wearing an opalescent hula skirt.

We became increasingly, recklessly brazen about videotaping locations, a development that begged for repercussions. Wagner graced the bar at the legendary acoustic listening room Anderson Fair. ("It's a bust!" cried a woman at the counter.) He led a line of Buddhas on an altar at Tien-Hou Temple, a feat made easier by the serendipitous exit of every other person from the building. He paid his respects at the grave of Howard Hughes, rested at the Water Wall, and interacted with public statuary installations, from Joan Miró to gnomes at Allen Center.

He surveyed Houston's skyline from the top of a pyramid (which both humans had to climb) at Watermelon Flats. He visited Wagner's Hardware, a hodgepodge of commercial signage (including the neon roach of Holder's Pest Control), and just about every folk art environment within Loop 610.

He stopped well past midnight to greet fellow statuary at a flower shop near the Medical Center; the workers never broke their gaze nor their silence, even when we moved Wagner next to a mural across the street. On Allen Parkway just outside of downtown, he cruised the darkened skyline while a member of the Montrose Singers boomed, "We fly through the night sky, showing our fat thighs, picking up dead guys, whoa hoya ta ho." During peak drag-queen hours, in the aftermath of the bars' closing, Wagner took a breather, perched on an upturned cup at Charlie's Coffee Shop.

These activities drew nothing more than the occasional look. Even when my boom box blared Wagnerian opera in covered walkways at Rice University, no one confronted us. A high-decibel broadcast of "Ride of the Valkyries" did lure a staffer out the door of the physics building just as I was panning the camera to the bust, which Doc had moved behind my back from a niche to the left of the door to one on the right. The staffer caught sight of the lens and disappeared. On tape, it looks as if Wagner has opened the door himself and glided to the niche.

The knick-knacky décor of a barbecue place inspired us to do a little taping before indulging in lunch. We introduced Wagner to a stuffed armadillo and, under the scowling eye of a well-aged customer, let our companion rest briefly among the iced longnecks. Once our attention turned to the menu and the order line, a managerial-looking man approached and asked if we'd been photographing a statue in the ice.

As thoughts of health code violations raced through my mind, he requested to see the statue. Doc produced it from his black traveling bag. The manager took it, thanked us, and walked away – until my outburst and Doc's significantly calmer explanation, laden with references to the Orange Show, caused the manager to finally, really look at what was in his hands – clearly not the property of the barbecue joint. He quickly handed it back. When we arrived at the cash register, the cashier said our check had been taken care of. Wagner had bought us lunch.

Another first in the Wagner travels (besides being accused of stealing his own property) was drawing commentary by a passer-by. A man with a very large dog was struck by the tableaux: a man wearing a ponytail and a black "Death to the Pixies" T-shirt holding up, in his left hand, a bust, against the backdrop of a house stuccoed with plaster cast face masks, and sighting the scene through a camera held in his right hand. "You're clearly doing something very strange indeed," the onlooker announced in a vaguely British accent, divining that it must not have anything to do with the Pixies, "because you display a certain antipathy to them." We explained the nature of our mission, whereupon the visitor burst out, "Why would you do that? He was a *terrible* person!" (Which, in case it needs explaining, is exactly the point.) This is the only time that anyone has approached Wagner's visual chronicler to ask what the hell he's doing.

This holding forth on the composer's merits didn't make it into the video, but several others did. One interviewee mouthed off about advances in composition since Wagner's time and feigned the bust's lunging at her throat. Another compared him to a dry martini ("rough at first, but you learn to love it").

We chanced upon most of them, but actively sought out two other video subjects. The first was a museum preparator with a supply of poly-vinyl acetate. She reattached Wagner's head for good, we hoped, while I played R.E.M. in the background. (After his surgery, an obnoxious bar patron mistook him for Thomas Jefferson.)

The second was Herman the German, whose Austin-based band Das Cowboy was playing at Dan Electro's Guitar Bar. Herman semi-polkaed about the stage in a German World War I uniform while playing smoking, high-reverb guitar ("full-tilt surf polka" and "rockabilly twang" are the two descriptions he used). Doc's insistence that we get him in the video caused me to spend the last two songs of evening mentally pruning grammatical errors from a request *auf Deutsch*. "*Entschuldigen Sie, bitte, darf ich Sie ein paar Fragen stellen, wenn Sie ein bisschen Zeit haben?*" I asked confidently, flawlessly, as the band broke down the stage. "I moofed he-yah in nahnteen-fiffty-et," he replied, confessing that he no longer speaks German. He went before the camera anyway, after lengthy negotiation, and ended up being the only person on the tape who took the endeavor seriously.

The Orange Show event turned out to be beside the point. Hindered by the hysteria-producing effects of protracted sleep deprivation and a day without eating, we finished shooting less than an hour before the video's scheduled premiere. Only a handful of loyal friends and intriguing strangers weathered daunting heat and our inexperience with the borrowed, barely functional slide and overhead projectors. Statues in attendance included Ludwig van Beethoven, who watched the video with his nose practically pressed against the monitor, and a lovely, multi-piece Asian figurine.

Due to a communal slip of the mind, the event had been scheduled too early in the evening, so we juggled the order of activities (beginning with the Looney Tunes cartoon, *What's Opera, Doc?*) on the spot in the hopes that the sun would begin to set. The sky remained too light to do justice to the gossipy slideshow Doc had put together introducing Wagner ("Guilty pleasures: Abba"). Any semblance of coherence and explicability disintegrated. The guest of honor was presented to his adoring public in a shopping cart.

He retired, uncomplaining, to the black camera bag, while we mere mortals took long-awaited nourishment at Ninfa's on Navigation. Wagner's last view of Houston came from the upper deck of the Orange Show, where he and a cardboard cutout of Orange Show creator Jeff McKissack stood behind flickering citronella candles, under a waning moon.

Wagner Bites the Big Apfel

Seventeen days, six cities, five residences,
three states, two people, and a bust

I used to say that traipsing all over Houston in 100-degree peak humidity in the summer of 1992 with a beat-up bust of Richard Wagner was the stupidest thing I'd ever done. I didn't know then how I would end up spending half of October.

It started when my sister Karen sent a smart-ass postcard to Doc, *Compendium* pen pal, and caretaker of the far-roaming, well-worn star of booklet and video. (She'd received a set of his Wagner booklets, which I'd ordered as her birthday present.) Almost as a throwaway, she'd scribbled the postscript that sealed our fate: "This is Wagner's first invitation to New York."

We showed her: We showed up.

Brooklyn-based Elaine graciously supplied weekend accommodations, rain gear, directions, advice, and, when her schedule allowed, companionship (both entertaining and bemused). We invaded her home for a few days, cleared out when her roommates returned from their double life as rural antique purveyors (an occupation that had strewn their architecturally quirky city digs with weird old signs, such as *Danger: High Voltage* on the front door), and came back shamelessly once they left.

It was the 180-degree-turn tour from the start. Turn right; turn left; look at a map; turn around. "Someone sucked out our brains when we landed," Doc explained near the end of the first week, "And would they please give them back???" I specialized in misreading maps of the subway line, while Doc researched combinations and permutations of wrong turns on the route between the subway station and Elaine's apartment. For which we had written directions. Wagner was no help. (As usual, he just went along for the ride.) In fact, in tandem with Doc's PXL camera, he became quite a pain in the lower back.

Locals, on the other hand, were quick to offer assistance, sometimes before we consciously sent out signs of needing it. The first time we strayed from Elaine's prescribed path from the subway, a Brooklyn resident gave us a whole new route and the wish, "good luck." He'd routed us alongside a mammoth, menacing housing project, which we had to cut back through, well after one in the morning, to get to home-away-from-home; we made it without incident, beyond comments about white people.

Caught in a rainstorm unprepared, Doc and I took shelter under a shop canopy while Elaine walked around Fifth Avenue in search of umbrellas for sale. Within minutes, two men approached us, one in a suit and one holding a cardboard box. "Wanna buy an umbrella?" the suited one asked, while his assistant handed over the goods for a mere $3 each. When she rounded the corner empty-handed, she was amused to see that the mountain had come to Mohammed.

On a bus, a well-dressed man told Elaine which line runs up to St. John the Divine, asked where we were all from, and launched into Houston jokes, late-80s vintage (Doc and Wagner's Arizona hometown being a less attractive target for potshots), which he was still telling when we made our way up to the front of the bus and disembarked.

Elaine led us on foot from Brooklyn across the Brooklyn Bridge to the base of the World Trade Center, where Wagner met the person who had instigated this endeavor, and Doc interviewed anyone who'd ask him about his camera. (It looks like a sleek, high tech device but is really a discontinued Fisher-Price toy. It records audio and visuals at phenomenally high speed on metal cassette tape and produces grainy, b&w images with the clarity of surveillance footage.) We didn't attract much attention; the ongoing street theater routinely upstaged anything we were up to. Wandering through the financial district, we crossed paths with a nontraditional Columbus Day parade (complete with sloganned caskets) protesting Old World evils perpetrated on New World soil. A few blocks up at Trinity Church, one of the parade onlookers was a middle-aged woman in a silver lamé tea-length dress and tennis shoes. In the East Village we came across a man in a foam refrigerator, who was promoting a film about a household appliance gone demonic. In the West Village, a pair of Pakistani capitalists treated Doc's request for a photo ID for Wagner with dead earnestness. They described the available formats in ludicrous detail, and kept trying to guide us to one requiring a social security number, which we would have had to make up, a fact they pointed out nonjudgmentally. I made up a year of birth and forged his signature; Doc held the subject still for his photo.

We escorted Wagner to the top of the World Trade Center and the crown of the Statue of Liberty, where a few French tourists seemed moderately puzzled. (We left him behind for the late-night jaunt up the Empire State Building.) For the price of two damned good Broadway tickets, we took him up in a helicopter ride that circled Lady Liberty and the roofs of Manhattan. We made a pilgrimage to the Algonquin Hotel, where the doorman's fascination for the camera prompted him to spill stream-of-consciousness gossip about the celebrities (now mostly actors) he has encountered, and how much they tipped him.

With Elaine again in tow, we stumbled upon a Chinese-American Buddhist shrine with a multi-shelved tray stacked with bottles of cooking oil; ferreted out an industrial plastic store with petroleum byproducts in every imaginable craft size and shape (including that ubiquitous gal about town, Ms. Liberty); and walked into our own shaggy dog story. Elaine had heard about the Earth Room installation at the Dia Foundation in Soho; this, from a friend whose taste and opinion she trusts and values. She thought it was around the corner from the plastic shop, but we walked up to Houston St. without seeing it. (Any further would have been Noho, you see, and no longer the correct neighborhood.) She went into a shop (which sold Hawaiian decorating items) for directions. The saleswoman didn't know, but ran outside to ask an artist who was working in the street. He directed us to the same block a few streets over. We combed that block without locating our destination. We ducked into a gallery and, stepping carefully over and around an installation scattered across the floor, asked a receptionist for directions. She didn't know the address, but described what she thought the building looked like. The one that matched her description had, at the side of the doorway, a small engraved address plate that said something like "EARTH ROOM INSTALLATION DIA FOUNDATION (1977) RING BUZZER." We rang, waited for the lock to buzz open, climbed a flight of stairs, and walked into a suite with three rooms filled a couple of feet high with black dirt. We looked at each other and burst out laughing. Doc later wished he'd tossed Wagner onto the middle of the dirt.

In the Museum of the Moving Image, next to the Paramount Astoria studios where early Marx Brothers and W.C. Fields films were shot, our inspection of an exhibit on the history and development of movie and special effect makeup was disrupted by the cacophonous clamoring of visitors in the room behind ours. The throng, which turned out to be a gang of highly vocal developmentally disadvantaged adults, quickly entered our midst, and one of them appointed Doc his personal answer man.

Our midweek home was the cushy midtown apartment of an opera singer chum who was off working in Europe. Wagner met a somewhat more diminutive bust of Mozart, and we met the mesmerizing wonders of Manhattan cable, from insurance experts with the sartorial flair of tax accountants to psychics, psychics, and more psychics. The first was the Psycho Psychic, who told obnoxiously unfunny jokes and insisted on wearing a penis-nosed set of glasses before "answering" questions from viewers calling in. I got through to one – an adenoidal woman named Dr. D, who advised me, as she did all the other callers, that we were moving into sensitive matters that should be discussed in private, such as on her private line for free the next night. (I did call, but a machine answered. Instead of leaving a message, I tied up the phone line trying to get through to the blues-loving psychic then on the air, for the entire duration of his show.) About the time of night that the psychic shows wound down, Channel J kicked in, filled with commercials for 976 numbers with suffixes like TWAT and PISS (the promo for which actually simulated golden showers from an off-screen source) and interrupted by the occasional stripping segment. "They can't do that on TV, can they?" Doc would repeatedly cry out, whereupon the unbelievable would proceed to take place on screen.

These things have a way of mushrooming, especially when this particular trio converges, and the itinerary expanded well beyond its original parameters. Doc and Wagner met quite a parade of my friends and relations. On the East Coast alone, there were sister Karen (who serenaded Wagner with "Why Don't We Get Drunk and Screw" in an ultimate dive called the Village Idiot, where a beautiful young bartendress pitched ice at customers as a behavior control technique); my favorite aunt (who pointed out a New Jersey butcher shop whose owner refused to clear out his regular customers in advance of a shopping trip by one Mr. Nixon); my pal since grade school Hugh (who was in the States on holiday from investment-advising a London-based Saudi Arabian sheik), and Hugh's and my mutual friends (who conducted a Jack-terrier-enhanced tour of the New York hamlet that gave the tuxedo its name).

And that was just in the first week. We moved our party to Dallas, where every other member of my immediate family would sooner or later come within Wagner's ambit. The first main stop was Dealey Plaza, one of the primary reasons for Wagner & Co.'s return to Texas, the other being free entry into the Houston Grand Opera's dress rehearsal of *Lohengrin*. We couldn't find a convertible, so I drove my trusty standard Corolla (gunning at 40 mph, despite being trapped in 1st gear since I had no third hand to shift gears with a load of traffic on its tail) down Elm Street holding Wagner out the open passenger window, while Doc recorded the event from the vantage point of the grassy knoll. He made the acquaintance of a pair of conspiracy freaks, who seemed not the slightest bit perplexed by our little tableau.

From there it was on to the State Fair, escorted by my sister-in-law and adored nephew, where we waited in vain for Big Tex to speak (he dwarfs Wagner in size, but hardly in stature; certainly not in ego), searched without success for any remnant of the freak shows of yesteryear, and recorded Wagner's fortune being intoned by the magical mechanical Zoltar. I also paid a visit on the Daughters of the American Revolution to seek out information that a San Francisco-based friend has been needing to gain membership, for which she is genealogically qualified. The membership director not only answered my friend's question (thereby easing the entry into the DAR of an outspoken, sexual-aid-designing dyke), but gushed a wish that she could help me obtain membership as well. Maturity and politeness controlled my facade. If she only knew, on both counts.

Before heading south, we stopped outside the home of the president of the Dallas Wagner Society. Doc has been sending her Wagner booklets anonymously, one at a time, and we thought a photo of the bust at her own home might finally get a response.

She was indirectly connected with the highlight of the Houston leg of the trip: a lecture at the Goethe-Institute about Wagner's relationship with animals. When we entered the sparsely attended auditorium, I was startled by the sight of a mailing tube addressed to the speaker with a return address of our last Dallas stop. I alerted one of the Institute employees that Wagner was present, and she suggested telling the speaker. "Wagner's here," I shouted out to a well-dressed woman who appeared to be in her sixties. She looked at Doc and seemed to be focusing on his ponytail. "Not him," I said, "He's here," and pointed at the black canvas bag in which the bust travels. The woman lit up and exclaimed, "Are you the people who've been videotaping that bust all over town?" She knew who we were. She'd read the Wagner Houston diary I'd written for the *Houston Press*. ("I could have kicked myself! I wish I had done that!") So had other people in the audience. My Institute pal fashioned a pedestal from a stool draped with fabric, and Wagner served as visual aid for the speech, as well as the punchline for the docent's joke about how far she'd fallen since speaking in

Chicago alongside a multi-thousand dollar likeness of the composer. "Do you call this performance art?" she asked us breathlessly at the evening's end, after holding forth, wine glass in hand, on camera next to the guest of honor.

Not everyone reacted so smoothly to the Master's unannounced return. At a party for the Orange Show, the folk art environment at which Wagner had made his Houston debut, the assistant director was unnerved when she spotted us. A university student friend of hers had been asking how to get in touch with Doc, and there he was. Seeker and sought spoke later that evening. The student had been assigned to choose a photographer whose work she admired and emulate it. She'd chosen Doc (who, it should be pointed out, uses a thrift-store Instamatic). The focus of her pictures, which she would present before her classmates at the University of Houston, was a loaf of bread from an upscale health food store. Each battered in its own way (the loaf had its innards partially kicked out), bust and bread met in broad daylight.

To fill some of the time before a return gig of Herman the German – a hell of a guitarist who dresses in a fake WWI outfit and plays heavily reverbed rockabilly twang/full tilt surf polka, not to mention strangely accented Gene Vincent covers – we headed down to Galveston. There, Doc became obsessed with portraits of the Three Stooges and Dan Quayle, composed entirely, and frighteningly accurately, of naturally colored slivers of rice straw. They were in the Straw Art Museum, in the upper gallery of an ancient drug store on 23rd St., along with an array of celebrity portraits (Tony Danza??) and scads of letters from well-known people all across the country whom the Indian-born proprietor had been pestering with his handiwork.

That evening, after three guys in a truck pushed us out of the sandbank I'd driven into, zine subscribers staged a "zilch" in Wagner's honor. In an unlit room, they set fire to a braided dry-cleaning bag, which dripped audibly (hence the name "zilch") into steaming dry ice.

En route to the airport, we returned to the scene of the perceived crime: the barbecue joint that had accused us last summer of shoplifting Wagner. Doc signed the register, "Richard Wagner," and wrote under comments, "Thanks for not arresting me this time." Just as all good things must come to an end, so must stupid ones. Besides, we had to go back to work to pay off the freshly minted credit card charges. Or rather, two of us did. As did his flesh-and-blood predecessor, Wagner has a way of dodging the bill.

Wagner Visits Twin Peaks

The speed of e-mail is a double-edged sword: You can pound out a thought and dispatch it immediately, before your proverbial better judgment kicks in and evaluates the likely consequences of your words. I'll be staying a quarter of a mile from Snoqualmie Falls, I emailed Doc, pen pal, fellow prankster, and tenacious fan of the several-year-old inscrutable television series that focused on said falls in its opening credits. As soon as I hit the send key, I felt the puncture of self-impaling. The response was inevitable: Doc knew someone who would *love* to go along. He wasn't talking about himself, either. I knew all too well whom he meant: his amanuensis, his alter ego, his prop, his excuse for no end of outrageousness and annoyance, his blasted, busted up bust of Wagner, back *just in time!* from a photo tour of Germany.

I didn't bring the matter up again, because I knew that was one thing I could rely on Doc to do. Sure enough, during my layover in the Phoenix airport, he asked, stressing that I could say no, if I would take Wagner along for photographing at *Twin Peaks*' sites. Of course I agreed;[30] I'd left just enough room in the carry-on bag for this eventuality. Wagner was laid to rest, wrapped in the swath of fake ermine we'd bought three years ago for the crowning finish of our video, *Wagner's Houston*, atop a black satin bra.

I was heading northwesterly to visit separate but equal contingents of pals, a couple known as the Two Daves[31] and the endlessly extended family of the mischievous J. The trip was marked by magnificently clear skies and more than my minimum daily requirement of weird, not all of which involved a stowaway.

License plate frame: "Warning: I brake for lattes"

In Seattle, a pedestrian traffic jam caught our attention on a corner outside a gay mall on Broadway. The cause was a more-than-foot-long puppet of a warthog with a microphone, telling drop-dead stupid jokes in a low-pitched snarl. I was entranced. It called for a volunteer with a

---

[30] Yeah, right, like I was going to say no, after already having lugged that bust all over hot, humid Houston in a car with malfunctioning air-conditioning; invested upwards of $75 to accompany it on a helicopter ride over Manhattan; talked my parents into putting it (and us) up for a night; and held it out the passenger window while I drove by Dealey Plaza and Doc conversed with conspiracy freaks in the park.

[31] …whose refrigerator is littered with magnets of the Michelangelo sculpture and his sizable wardrobe, which include high heels and a few other cute little items cribbed from a set intended for Venus de Milo.

high school education. "Kathy," said one of the Daves. "Kathy," said the other Dave. "Kathy," said another man in the crowd. The warthog asked if I believed he could read my mind. "Sure!" I said. "I need a little more cynicism!" he barked. "Okay, I don't!" I complied.

He put me through elaborate mental gymnastics that led to silently accumulating a number, a country, and an animal. Before he announced my results, he prepared the crowd to ante up with cash if he succeeded. One of the Daves put a dollar in the tray under the stage. "A deposit!" he shrieked approvingly. "Is the number four?" "Yes." "Is the country Denmark?" "Yes." "Is the animal kangaroo?" "Yes." The warthog proclaimed that he'd read my mind. "No, I was sending to you," I disagreed. "Oh! A clairvoyant!" he countered. Everyone laughed, a few people dropped coins in the tray, and the warthog demanded that we tell him a riddle. "Why is a raven like a writing desk?" I asked. "Oh, Lewis Carroll!" he growled, and began reciting a gravelly "Jabberwocky."

I wanted to take the warthog home, but that would have involved a tall, nice-looking young man in a striped *Where's Waldo?* shirt. Inspired by this incident (…and by Annette Funicello warbling a beach party song…), Dave the Younger and I capped the ensuing meal with a high-spirited food fight that escalated from tossing French fries to shooting ice into finger hockey goals, while monkey-in-the-middle Dave the Elder quietly enjoyed a cigarette and a Bombay gin martini.

I took Wagner, shrouded in his fake ermine, along on a day trip to Vancouver. Signs at the Canadian border required declaring any offensive weapons. We passed without incident, even without mentioning our strange cargo. Wagner did catch attention, however, at the troll under the Aurora bridge,[32] though only along the lines of, "Hey, wow, that's really

[32] Point of scale: its left hand clutches an honest-to-God VW Beetle.

weird." No one noticed him, however, alongside the sculpture of people waiting under a bus shelter in Fremont, which changes clothes and signage according to whims of passers-by. I didn't even bother to bring him out at the house covered with Jello molds.

At lunch on the golf course in Snoqualmie, C., son of J., announced that he wouldn't be going along to photograph Wagner at various *Twin Peaks* sites after all, because he embarrasses easily. (This from the man whose initial reaction to Wagner was that we should roll him in Saran Wrap and put him in the river in front of the mill.) Despite his comment, I left the greatest composer of all time on our table. As the meal progressed, C. tore off a strip of his napkin, dabbed it with ketchup, and stuck it into the hole in Wagner's forehead.[33] The rest of the napkin he folded into a long bandage, which he wrapped around W's head. After fastening the ends with a paperclip J. fished from her purse, he spooned ketchup onto the spot over the hole.

"C. is perverse," his father said that evening, with a smile.

After lunch, without prompting, C. nonetheless facilitated shots of Wagner before the diner, against mountain peaks and in the middle of the highway, where, unfortunately, no danger threatened him. At least, not there. That the Angel of Destruction was keeping the bust in its sights, however, was brought to our awareness in my friends' idyllic backyard. Resting on an umbrella-topped wrought iron table, Wagner was lingering over a coffee cup and a pack of smokes when I spied a nook just his size in a bower made of apple tree branches. He fit, but was too heavy to stand by himself, so I stood him on the ground. A few minutes later, a terrific crash broke out. A gust of wind had lifted the umbrella, which had knocked

[33] He took a tumble into the Rio Grande, see, after attempting *Liebestod* to impress a statuette named Gretchen.

over the table and jettisoned everything that had been on it down the deck stairs, which were now littered with dirt and shards from the flower pot that had doubled as ashtray. The felt beneath Wagner's pedestal was wet. He'd moistened himself, and no wonder! I laid him on his back to dry, next to the house, went inside, and (sorry, Doc!) forgot about him. Until someone asked, several hours later, "Why is Wagner sunbathing on the deck?" J. and I related the tale of Wagner's near-demise to her husband and son. "Odd that gust of wind," said the first. "Must have been a Bach draft," said the second.

Wagner did make it to Snoqualmie Falls,[34] thanks to J. and her husband, who was charmed by the whole Wagner nonsense ("You talk just like your zine!" he exclaimed my first night in his house) and dreamed up shot after shot. Through his efforts, the plaster menace found its way to the streets of Roslyn, which had earlier that week lost its communal livelihood as location for *Northern Exposure*. Wagner posed in front of the KBHR studio, the Brick, and the doctor's office.

Outside Roslyn's Cafe, a clerk I'd seen at the hardware store walked by as I lowered Wagner[35] to change the film in my camera. "Oh," he said, taking a good look at my charge. "I thought it was an ice cream cone."

My carry-on bag triggered concern at the Seattle airport. "Do you have a statue in there?" a security guard asked. I unzipped the bag and pointed at the fake ermine. She unrolled the cloth, got a look at Wagner's battered

---

[34] And to the Snoqualmie Log, which I found on my own reconnaissance. "Guess this makes you the Wag-Log Lady," said my personal life commentator Rex.

[35] How to make a Wagner photo: (1) Become acquainted with Doc. (2) When he offers you the bust, which he will, sooner or later, especially if you live near or travel to really cool places, take it. (3) Hold it in your non-dominant hand and stretch your arm out. (4) Hold a camera in your free (i.e., dominant) hand. (5) Press the button. Viola (sic)!

visage, carefully rolled it up, all without saying a word.

Back in Houston, my friend who'd agreed to give me a ride home greeted me with the news that he'd parked at Ludwig's castle – meaning one of the photos of architectural wonders the airport posts as aids for locating cars in the parking lot. The door opening was irresistible. As the last act of the trip, my camera captured the tireless model next to an image of his royal patron's best-known folly. Visual, that is.

Running Around in the Rain with a Romanian Poet

When Andrei Codrescu was in Houston to give a speech for the Unitarians, he spent the afternoon on a weird tour conducted by... me. (How this came about was that the event organizer, who is a subscriber to my zine, showed up in my office one morning and asked how I would like to be involved in the speaker's off-stage time. You people may not be numerous, but you're sure as hell well-placed.)

We had to excuse our way through a swarm of passengers from a retirement home van to get a good look at the Beer Can House. Using a disposable camera someone had given him, I got a particularly mischievous shot of Andrei as directed, looking back through a sea of the elderly.

In the cemetery where Howard Hughes is buried, we gawked at a skyline framed by beautiful, broken statues of angels. "He was a Caprrricorrrn," Andrei commented, looking at the millionaire's pie wedge in the family plot. Rain started falling. We ran for the car. My passenger looked up, threw an arm skyward and proclaimed, "This is perrrrfect!"

At the Flower Man's House, he held the disposable camera out the car window to snap a photo of a plastic Dracula head impaled on a stick. By the time we reached the Orange Show, the force of the rain and wind obliterated the usefulness of my oversized umbrella, which was reminding Andrei of a lightning rod.

Between stops, we traded elaborate anecdotes that would have justified running a tape recorder for four hours. Somebody sent me Baby Jesus for Easter, I said. He met the challenge, and countered that a blow-up doll with a vibrating penis, switched on, once (I guess this is the sort of thing that doesn't happen twice) flew out of a package in the office of *Exquisite*

Corpse, the poetry journal he edits. The same person also sent the journal dirt from a grave and a 40s-vintage toaster with bread crumbs inside.

As the afternoon wore on, I tipped him off to my own uncomfortable history with the venue for his speech, an Episcopal high school stage; the last time I'd been there, producing a concert for the very same Unitarians, I'd thought the theater director knew the performers were gay – a detail that escaped everyone's notice until the week of the concert, when news of it clamored up the hierarchy to the Bishop and the diocesan chancellor, and triggered the negotiating chess game of my life. Which I won.

Andrei's reaction to the story was that he'd been gay a time or two, so he should change the topic of his speech to "Men I Have Slept With and Why I Did It."

We closed out the afternoon in an atmospheric Montrose bar overlooking a huge live oak. I gave him the choice of the inner-city journalists' hangout, which is a somewhat yuppified but very nice bar in a Mexican restaurant, or a strange, kinda divey gay bar. "Therrre's no choice," he responded, and he was right.

An inscrutable and interminable traffic jam trapped us in River Oaks, which inspired Andrei to speculate about what goes on inside the mansions we were crawling past. Not much, in his musings, and certainly not sex; at that moment he said people were sitting in darkened rooms at the backs of the houses, fearful that servants would drop trays of hot food on their heads.

I delivered him into the hands of the Unitarians, who interrupted his quest for bourbon with a cocktail-as-euphemism-for-wine party. Likewise, I found only light sustenance in the speech and dinner afterwards, in comparison to the afternoon's close-range, full-blast raconteur-ism. When exhaustion drove me from the table, Andrei thanked me for a most amazing weird tour, and I went home very happily indeed.

Hand-of-God Coda

At the end of the post-speech book signing, the wife of the aforesaid nearly-sacked theater director, also a school employee and the person in charge of locking up that evening, came up to Andrei for an autograph. She started to tell him the saga of the gay concert crisis. I interrupted that I'd already told him. She said there was a new punchline. When this church event came up, she was sure it had to be clean and there was no way the speech could cause a problem for the school. The day the school signed the contract, *All Things Considered* aired Andrei's musings on the president's penis. "Face it, Janet; it's karma!" I yelled.

The Blessed Visitation

Alot of things show up in my mailbox that would never arrive in anyone else's, but even I am broadsided by what surfaces a couple of days into Passover on a dark, rainy April morn. It's heralded by a yellow slip marked "parcel," which confuses me because the post office usually leaves a key in the box that matches up with a locker containing the posted goodie. The postal worker emerges from the back room hoisting on her shoulder a carton the size of a toddler's coffin. My first reaction is terror. The need for checking with a bomb squad suggests itself. I stare at the return address until the point of origin sinks in. The filter between conscious mind and wild-eyed rambling shuts down and I blurt, "Baby Jesus is in this box!" The postal worker blinks at the obvious sign of possession and I am compelled to answer, "I'm not kidding! Baby Jesus is in this box!"

The Annunciation

I had been warned eight months earlier that he might be coming. In the Nevada desert, where a Ladies' Fetish & Taboo Society contingent had traveled for fun and games with the San Francisco Cacophony Society, a ringleader named Michael Michel (who'd been sending correspondence under the name Genevieve) had alerted us of Baby Jesus. The visitor'd slipped away from a creche in front of a church in the Midwest and had been touring the country, all the while writing letters to the folks back

home. Maybe he'd like to come to Houston someday, our informant had suggested. "Every traveling statue in the country is going to come to your mailbox," retorted Doc, who should know; he has himself placed a beat-up bust of Richard Wagner in it.

The package will not fit into the car. I put it in the trunk and whisk it homeward. What am I going to do with this? I wish I'd got some advance notice so I could have planned an appropriate event to honor His coming. But then, the Lord works in mysterious ways.

I'm bombarded by a slew of outrageous turns of thought that beg for lightning. Nothing compares to the serenity a girl has driving around secure in the knowledge that the savior of the world is in her trunk. All the post offices in the world and He has to walk into mine. I guess this makes me blessed among women. And what does this mean as Omen? Personal rebirth? Grace arrived in my post office box. I got Baby Jesus for Easter; what did you get? What would Joseph Campbell have made of this?

The first call goes to Rex. I have him on the line while opening the package; if anything goes awry, I want someone to be able to phone 911 on my behalf. I slit the tape open with a steak knife. A large note is taped on top. "Kathy — He's here! Michael." Carefully, nervously, I peel back a section of the butcher-block swaddling. A beatific face with eerie blue eyes and blond curls peeks out. I scream and jump back, immediately overcome by a nearly 25-year-old memory of a night of terror in a Bavarian guesthouse, when a wax baby Jesus in a glass coffin so unnerved my siblings and me that our highly irritated father had to sleep in our room. I can not continue this alone. The youngster stares out sightlessly from the wrapping paper while Rex and I ponder the proper course of action. Taking him to the gay bars is my first idea. "The people that go there have conflicted self-images and are already on the edge," he cautions, "and seeing this might push them right over, with possible Manson-esque consequences." Within 30 minutes, and less than a third as many phone calls, a probable, more onlooker-friendly schedule emerges.

First things first: a spa. He's had a long journey and would no doubt appreciate rejuvenation. Once out of the brown paper, He loses a bit of His holy terror. His back is flat, papoose-like; His little hands are stretched out just about the perfect distance for a cat's cradle; a large chunk is missing from His golden halo, but who among us cannot say the same thing? Our benefactor, the proprietress of the Institute for Natural Therapeutics, places Him in a cheery innertube, puts a scrub mitt on His left hand, and nestles Him into a hydrotherapy tub.

Then it's back in the box, and back to the trunk. Maundy Thursday and Good Friday are coming, a time with a high probability for traumatizing the Visitor. He'll emerge again on Easter Sunday.

In the meantime, I pass the word. When I alert Val, she declares me to be that from which quantum physics emanates. The concept is flattering. It occurs to me that the highest and best use of my life will probably be writing my autobiography.

Baby Jesus and the Briar Patch

Easter Sunday, 7:30-ish, a cadre assembles with me at a piano/wrinkle bar called the Briar Patch: Rex Celestis, Fellow Buddy David, Lizzie-Ba, Paolo, and John-the-Not-So-Terminally-Weird. Rex and I have feet at sub-zero temperatures. Gin-and-tonic builds some Dutch courage, and the bar's owner provides the rest. When he stops by the table, no doubt to check out the straight riff-raff, his regulars among us get him to agree to play the piano later. John informs him that we're expecting a special guest and requests a specific blasphemous song parody. "You're not Christians, are you?" owner Wayne asks. "As a matter of fact," Rex starts, while I'm contemplating announcing that we have the ur-Christian among us, "The guest we're waiting for is Jewish." I run to the car and free Baby Jesus. John props him up in a chair. "You people are sicker than I thought," Wayne says, disappearing.

When the live music begins, we commandeer the stools that ring the clear-plastic-lidded piano. Wayne is sitting at the left hand of the Visitor. A black hat with big pink bunny ears makes the rounds and eventually comes to rest atop BJ. It lends a certain resemblance to a version of Him popular in Mexico. Unaffected by the scene, Wayne pounds out show tune after show tune, frequently mutated by sexually perverse lyrics. He segues into sacrilege. "Has Anybody Seen My Gal?" is revamped to apply to Jesus. John sings along; apparently it's a Briar Patch standard:

Five-foot-nine from Palestine, changes water into wine,
has anybody seen JC?
He's so neat, he's so cool, he walks across my swimming pool;
has anybody seen JC?
If you see a 5'9 from Palestine covered in blood,

nail scarred hands, and crown of thorns, you can bet that he's the one.
He can preach, he can teach, he can wash those Baptists' feet;
has anybody seen JC?

Inspired, Lizzie-Ba screams out, "2, 4, 6, 8, time to transubstantiate!" After he recovers from obvious distaste at the pitch of a distaff voice, Wayne follows with, "Buddha loves me / This I know / For the Buddha Book tells me so."

When I trail Rex to the bar to pass on some thoughts, urgent at the time but now, as usual, lost to all memory, I realize the throng behind us is singing "Away in a Manger."

Gradually, strangers join the party. No one balks at the Presence, although some are curious about the empty glass I've placed in front of Him. "What's He drinking?" someone asks and is pleased by the misinformation that it's gin. (By this point, I've long since switched to bitters as tonic additive.)

Periodically Lizzie-Ba floats by my station to exude delight over the situation. There is something immensely cheering about seeing the Little One in this context, beneath the aegis of a huge glitter ball. It remains motionless, but Wayne does switch on a string of red Christmas lights that line the piano's interior. They flash off and on as we tap dance with quarters on the lid in time to "Tea for Two." The sparse population of the central cruise bar stares at our spectacle silently, uncomprehendingly.

Nothing we do triggers a lightning bolt. The only time we manage to draw ire is when Wayne shuts down the proceedings briefly and none-too-happily because Lizzie-Ba is attempting to stand on the piano. John helps her redirect her exuberance to the floor and they swoop, lunge, and dip with lots of flourishes of arm and leg. Gradually the flow of martinis into Nick-and-Nora-Charles-style glasses stops, and the Fun Couple goes home while the hour is still reasonable.

The rest of us display considerably less sense. We retire to the better-lit back room for Tarot readings, despite the protestations of a trio of well-voiced singers, who object to our taking Jesus away from the piano. He waves goodbye, not so much with His hands as with His entire body, when we finally get the Baby Jesus out of there in search of long-needed nourishment. Rex and BJ spend the rest of the evening supine, separated only by one letter of the alphabet (BJ in my trunk and Rex on the floor of David's truck); as David observes later, they're both reduced to cargo. It's 1:30 in the morning when I finally arrive home.

The Continuing Adventures of Baby Jesus

BJ's been on sabbatical. He's spent an extended chunk of 1993 taking a breather in his traveling case, a big old mailing carton that's usually shoved against the demi-wall that separates my kitchen and dining area. But the times he's come up for air, it's been choice.

During August, Special Paolo and I spirited him about the Bayou City in search of inscrutable photo opportunities. He graced an entrance to the Astrodome, the Beer Can House, and a downtown installation of alien children statues lining the banks of the bayou. (Stepping out of the car, holding up a statue, positioning the camera and running for it triggered a strange déjà vu. Oh, Doc....)

A photo of this has turned out to be great postcard and wall decoration material, especially with the caption, "Aliens march through downtown Houston providing proof of long-suspected link between ETs and the divine."

After this expedition, the box stayed in the trunk for a while, just in

case. Never can tell when a savior might come in handy.

On the figurative eve of Burning Man, I whiled a pleasant evening in the company of the Womyn of Inertia (a Kerrville Folk Festival campground), Val and Catherine. We gathered at a bar with the very real name of McGonigel's Mucky Duck to bask in the storytelling, extremely pleasant personality, and eye-popping guitar picking of LJ Booth. As the witching hour approached, LJ's tales rambled into the territory of bathtub shrines. He'd written a song about them, and sung it at some Catholic institution, and gone for beers afterward with a bunch of carousers who stunned him at the end of their bender by confessing that they were nuns. With background like that, some might say that LJ should have been forewarned about the hazards of this line of conversation. He wondered out loud whether Houston has any bathtub shrines. I yelled back that it does and I'd helped build one of them.

He wanted to talk to me, and said that if I had to go before the set was over, he'd shut things down right then. Promptly possessed by a vision of where this conversation was going to head, I let him finish his performance undisturbed, as much out of selfishness (I wanted to hear this entrancing man play as long as possible) as out of courtesy. I even allowed a respite of peace and fan greeting before making my approach.

"There's something behind your car that you need to see," I said. He and a sprawling entourage of, oh, let's say, women, trotted out the door to the vehicle behind his Volvo, which was, of course, mine. Out from the trunk came Baby Jesus. LJ immediately put his hands around the babe and transformed him into a makeshift hood ornament for the car behind mine, which was, of course, Val's. The existence of the Ladies' Fetish & Taboo Society was thereafter revealed to him. The wide-eyed, wild-eyed expression that came over LJ suggested he was having a bit more difficulty assimilating this turn of events than his enthusiastic patter indicated. After the assemblage went its merry ways under the waxing moon, it crossed my mind that the incident might well end up as an anecdote on the Kerrville Folk Festival stage, where LJ was headed for Labor Day.

A few weeks later Val was riding the Metro from National Airport to some job-related conference in Our Nation's Capital when a man lunged at her and announced that Jesus was coming! Chapter 7 of Revelations says so! Her first reaction was to blurt back: "No, he's not; he's in the trunk of a Volvo in Houston." Something about the intensity of the man's expression held her back.

He's not in the trunk of a Volvo, of course, and never was, at least not in Houston. He was once, as was just disclosed, in the trunk of a car behind a Volvo, and at this particular time that this phrase crossed Val's mind, was in a box in a kitchen in Houston. Picky, picky. We've decided we like the second, though, of "in the trunk of a Volvo." It's like being in the catbird seat and having an ace up your sleeve, with divine protection rolled up in the works, to boot. We commend the phrase to you. May it serve you well.

Baby Jesus Goes Bye-Bye

Baby Jesus' final official act during his stay on the Gulf Coast was very official indeed. At the instigation of a high-ranking county officer, who happens to be a subscriber to the *Ladies' Fetish & Taboo Society Compendium of Urban Anthropology*, he was waived through Family Law Center security (his anonymity assured by a coffin-sized packing box), entered the tunnel system that links the courthouses, and posed for photos next to a sign for Harris County Child Support.

The next day, it was back in the mail for the babe. The Christmas season had arrived; he'd been with me nine months, and the time just seemed right to ship him off to his next cross-country stop. I sent him to a stripper in New York City, whom the folks that sent him to me had suggested. I didn't send any advance warning, but figured she knew he was coming. After all, she is a professional.

What a Friend
We Have in Jesus

A social activist Unitarian named Paul and I have been on the periphery of each other's lives for years. Paul used to date a friend of mine until the morning he called her cat by another cat's name. He later caused a great commotion at a church Halloween party by arriving clad in a loincloth and crown of thorns, and dragging an extremely large cross into the courtyard. Shoulder-length hair, parted in the middle, and a full beard completed the startling illusion. I feared lightning would strike the assembly, but the gathering went un-singed, although we did hear that he was denied entry into Charlie's Coffee Shop, the after-hours regrouping point of many a lost soul (and drag queen) later that night. (Suffice to say that Paul does not fall within the parenthetical group, though whether he did, at that time, fall into the first-named category is up for debate, albeit pointless.)

Tucked away among such mundane offerings as a carriage ride through downtown and a custom-made branding iron, "a visit from the Prince of Peace" was on the list of live auction items at the church services fundraiser. The donor was the self-same Paul, still long of hair and beard. The minister himself oversaw the bidding for the item and pointed out the possibilities inherent in it, what with Maundy Thursday, Good Friday, and Easter coming up. "Easter" caught my attention; Easter was going to coincide with the birthday of a back-slid Catholic singer-comedienne named Marianne. Conscious thought ceased, some vast force took control, and when the bidding began, I was at the start. And at the finish.

The surprise guest arrived at the birthday girl's house after dark, with a full moon visible, just as her celebrants (mostly lesbian, a fact mentioned not out of any intrinsic importance, but to give the full context) were serving up a potluck dinner weighted toward brown rice and slightly overcooked veggies.

"Do you mind if I bring this in?" he asked, placing a modular cross atop an altar the party had assembled on the living room floor. Most of the women maintained a more than respectful distance; many of them were visibly unnerved but not, fortunately, Marianne, who'd done time delivering singing telegrams.

He introduced himself with a little song ("My name is Jesus; my father's Joe, hello, hello, hello. I walk on water; I heal the lame..."), absolved the guest of honor of her sins, and serenaded her with a lullaby from *Jesus Christ Superstar*, throughout all of which Marianne was inquiring somewhat loudly, "Who did this?!?" The party moved the cross onto the porch for a series of group photos and offered the visitor a beer, dinner, and a place to change his clothes, the first and third of which he accepted.

Five months later I saw Paul walk up to the bar at Munchies Classic Cafe. I approached him to say hi. He greeted me with a double-take. He'd just concluded that the woman singing on stage was not me, he explained, when he turned and saw the real me standing next to him.

A week later, on a Friday night, I dreamed of walking past Paul at a gathering and being startled by his clean-shaven and unattractively short-haired appearance. That next Sunday I was summoned to church unexpectedly by a minor crisis. Running through the courtyard I caught a glimpse of Paul. He didn't have a beard. I looked again. His hair was cut to mid-ear level. He did not look bad, however. I ran over to him and demanded, "I need to know when you did this; I dreamed two nights ago that you did this." He said he'd shaved Friday night and got a haircut on Saturday. "Jesus!" I shrieked, and exited.

Highway 7

ighway 7 is a state of being. You know you are there, but there is no independent verification of "there" being anywhere. You suspect you have been teleported into another realm.

Hot Springs, Arkansas. Rex Capricornus and I are headed for a day of rooting through mud and routing out crystals at the Coleman Mine, just a short drive outside of town. I recognize a wood frame farm from last year's trip. One of the tracks on the tape player goes out, which leaves a lot of the music up to our imaginations. The road winds and winds and winds and I begin to wonder why we are not there yet. We seem to have been driving for much longer than the trip I recall. I keep looking for the wholesale rock shop on the right side of the road, and it keeps not being there.

A road sign says this is Highway 7. Rex checks the official state highway map, which has absolutely no reference to this number. We started out on Highway 5, which quite clearly leads to our intended destination. We are puzzled. We are obviously on a highway that obviously exists, even if unbeknownst to the map-makers of the state of Arkansas. If Highway 7 isn't on the map, where is it?

We turn around. The road winds and winds and winds. I still recognize the wood frame farmhouse. Soon we are on Highway 5 again, and not long after that the wholesale rock shop decides to be on the right side of the road. The tape player

resumes playing all tracks.

Months and months later, Rex De Minimis (having unintentionally slimmed during a cold that got out of control) and I are dining in a Thai restaurant. The appetizers are cleared. We become engrossed in conversation. We simultaneously realize how long it has been since we have seen either food or a waiter. A very long time. The party next to us that was seated after we were is paying the bill and leaving. We have clearly returned from a bout of invisibility. Or, more likely, another trip down Highway 7. Our skills are obviously increasing. This detour occurred without benefit of automobile.

Perception is Everything

or

Seeing May Be Believing, But Hearing Isn't Necessarily

I've long suspected that your impression of a person can cause your ears to go deaf to the reality of their statements. I've been working for 12 years with an attorney who is an elder in the Church of Christ, and whose opinion of me is such that I could swear like a sailor[36] around him and he would not hear it. Granted, I haven't tested this theory, at least not with him, and not consciously. I have, however, unwittingly received confirmation of its validity from quite another bend in my circle of acquaintances.

The proof capped one of those bizarre sequences of events that no one ever foresees or intends but that simply spiral outward on their own recognizance. This one began at a Christmas in July party hosted by an astrologer and a desktop publisher / massage therapist / belly dancer.[37] Carols were on the CD player, turkey and trimmings were on the table, and a fully decorated tree was in the living room. The tree was the focus of the party, the point of deposit of beautifully wrapped – or rather, camouflaged – packages that would soon be circulating among the guests (who were

---

[36] i.e., talk naturally

[37] Pop quiz: which is the Aquarian?

fairly evenly split between metaphysicians and belly dancers).

The distribution was the party's main event. Each person had drawn a number on arrival and, in sequence, got to select a piece of the bounty – either by taking a package from beneath the tree or seizing a goody that had already been opened. Certain of the items had already passed into the legend of this party, because they have been given for several years: a

punching nun puppet, an unsightly blob of stone barely carved to resemble a pig, a gigantic wooden "7-11 Coming Soon" sign pried off a commercial building.

This year's haul yielded even more abominations: a Southern Belle doll lamp base, a Richard Simmons workout record, a penis-shaped water pistol. The last was most representative of the lot, which was weighted in the direction of adult novelty items. Even though I'd heard a blow-up sheep was supposed to be under the tree, I wasn't going to take any chances. When my turn came, I confiscated a lovely set of handmade runes that had slipped in somehow. They stayed with me for only a few rounds. Their departure sent me once again to the tree. Inside the bag I chose was a box. Inside the box was a giant[38] penis-shaped soap on a rope. Holding the shrink wrap in place[39] was a sticker with a name we'll call Mr. Thudwhacker.

[38] 'bout 8"

[39] Hermetically sealed for your protection?

This was an irritating development. What the hell was I going to do with this – thing? Foisting it off on another guest was unlikely and, in any event, my entourage was soon forced to flee by A/C-defeating heat and growing anti-social tendencies. In the car, one of us tried out a condom catapult. One of us gushed over her antebellum doll, whose bluish skin tone would soon inspire transformation into a zombie. One of us gloated over a CD of Hanna-Barbera sound effects. And one of us figured out what to do with Mr. T.

My rounds on the party circuit were not over for the night. I walked down the block to the home of Monsieur and Madame X. It being only around 11, the action was far from winding down. A couple of cases of beer were iced down in the drained hot tub. The "Springtime for Hitler" number from *The Producers* was being shown on the VCR for the benefit of a teenaged guest from Germany. I greeted everyone I recognized. When I saw the bathroom unoccupied, I excused myself and shut the door to the porcelain chamber. I opened the shower stall. I opened my purse. I hung a piece of rope and its anatomically correct burden from the shower head. I went back to the party long enough to provide a cover, then I went home.

I figured the sound of discovery would reach me without benefit of a telephone. The air was quiet all the next day, though. When I talked to Mssr. X late in the afternoon, he said nothing about it. I began to wonder. Could these people have been too wasted from the party to expend the energy to shower? Not out of the realm of possibility; who among us can say that we haven't been there?[40] Or could it be that it was he, and not she, who stumbled onto the sight and was stunned into silence?

I saw them that evening walking to a bar around the corner. Mme. X

---

[40] Be honest!

was friendly and smiling. She seemed clean enough. But she didn't blurt anything about a giant penis materializing in her shower or elsewhere. I wasn't going to ask. This one would be waited out.

Four days later she called me at work. Someone had left a hostess gift at her party, and she didn't know who to thank. She'd risen around three the next day and gone into the bathroom to take a shower, where she'd found a penis-shaped soap on a rope named Mr. Thudwhatever. "Did you keep the label?" I asked, even though she hadn't mentioned one. Yes, she said she had.

Her shower surprise had caused her to construct an elaborate analytical framework for identifying the benefactor, which she'd been mulling over for days. She was sure the item was costly, which eliminated a large segment of her friends from the running. She didn't think that many people knew her well enough to spend that much money on an anonymous gift. She had recently given a pair of soap lips to a singer named Lips as a birthday present. Lips wasn't that close a friend, but the overlap of substance and body parts theme put her at the top of the suspect list.

"Maybe this is like that Alfred Hitchcock episode in which everyone confesses to the murder so that it can't be pinned on any of them," I suggested. "Maybe we all did it."

That thought amused her and prompted an examination of my own status. Mme. X was sure I could have afforded the item. "But I can't see you going into a store and saying, 'I'd like to buy Mr. Thudpucker.'"

"No, you're right; I wouldn't do that," I agreed. "But it is the sort of thing that could fall into my hands."

She agreed. "And I can see you saying, 'I know. I'll take it to the X-es.'"

"You're right," I said. She started to return to her analysis. "You've hit it on the head," I said. She said she was going to have to ask Lips about this. I gave up.

Yes, Madame X. *I* did it. I tried to confess, but you wouldn't hear it. *I'm* the one who gave you Mr. Thudwhosit.

Then again, maybe not.

All the World's a Stage (Or Something)

The High Seas of Androgyny & Ambiguity Flood the High Plains

…and many live to regret it

The summer of '96 brought the Southwest premiere of *STEAK!* – a musical about cattle-rustling vegetarians, with a plot convoluted enough to have sprung from these pages. I played one of the rustlers – a lesbian "Indian" named Rainbow, who yearned for sexually confused Dusty Lou, who turned out to be the fiancée-by-arrangement of one of the ranchers we were ambushing (Dallas), who fell for Bruce, who was chained to the bar by the dominatrix saloonkeeper, who tumbled happily into a mèlange with the ranchers' chef and the rustlers' cook. The skinny little fella who made rancher Paris' "prairie dog" pop up its head was really rustler Bambi-Jo (raised by deer); Austin crossed over to the side of the rustlers after reconnecting with the only person for miles who understood his literary references: a freed slave from his daddy's plantation by name of Betty-Bob; and Houston, who forced his unwanted attentions onto the cows and the dyke, and turned out to be a rustler himself. Everyone ended up together, in a brawl, in the saloon.

Not surprisingly, such an endeavor attracted participants whose proclivities quickly overshadowed the machinations of the script. At the auditions alone I met women with names like Brandi and Laurel and Felicity. The one who really gave me pause was a long-haired pixie in a black body suit that laced up the sides from ankle to armpit. As she squeaked out the dominatrix's lines and whipped her leg over the head of the man reading Bruce, my reaction popped out unfiltered: "Tinker Bell on acid!"

The woman who got the part of the saloonkeeper was a resident of the suburbs, who squealed over Hello Kitty and other Sanrio products (she used a Pekkle baby bottle carrier as a pencil case) and worked for a company that sent costumed characters to children's parties. She took great delight in the disparity of her pastimes, as well as in combing through inner-city leather shops for her halter and riding crop. "Barney assistant by day, dominatrix at night!" she laughed.[41]

"I'm a Christian, but I'm open-minded!" was the watchword of the youngest cast member. Badly in need of a visit from the Clue Fairy was more like it, as one audience member put it. While obliviousness and flat, barely audible delivery might add a note of charm to some parts, they were completely at odds with her role, which was, unfortunately, my girlfriend. (After weeks of the band straining to hear her 20 feet away, she stunned all by wailing "Sunshine of Your Love" at a bar's karaoke night.) "I'm not going to kiss you!" she announced to me almost as many times as "I'm a virgin!" She succumbed nonetheless to sequential crushes on most of the unmarried (but not, as we all know, necessarily straight) males around. She

---

[41] The second act opened with her wiping bar glasses and giving the impression of receiving oral sex. Just before the act, the assistant stage manager would open a folding chair and place it by a hidden break in the curtains. As soon as he'd sit, various actors would lean over him and crouch to ogle the cutaway view of how the sex was simulated. She had the boot of her bent leg resting on the back of Bruce, who was on all fours, hidden from the audience's view by the bar. When the lights went up, he simply raised and lowered his back to move her leg and create the illusion. She added the sound effects. (Closing night, she barked.) When the effect stopped, the actors would take their places, and the ASM would fold up his chair and leave.

identified her object of the moment by punching him in the shoulder, or tossing a plastic cow at him, or asking me if it was obvious. "Repressed" was the politest phrasing of the uniform opinion.[42]

The obligatory mind-boggling coincidence came to light early in rehearsals, when I glanced at a resume lying on a chair and spotted a production I'd seen 22 years earlier, at the high school from which I had just graduated. That credit didn't belong to just anyone, of course. It belonged to the man cast opposite me, who pinched my butt, threw me into a kiss that started a brawl, konked me on the head with a gun, and dragged me around on stage. Not only were we two years apart in high school, but he also had something I'd wanted; as the police department public information officer who wrote up the arrest report, he knew the particulars of our high school choir director's murder. My informant proved to be an ongoing voice of doom, passing on news of calamities as they paraded across his beeper.

Midway through the run, he dreamed about me. He was sitting in a Scottish village pub when I walked in and everyone stood up. He was warned to stand, too, or risk being struck with lightning. "I know her," he scoffed. "No, you don't," he was told. "That's God." Being a beneficent

---

[42] Typical interchange: After she overheard me telling a band member that a mutual friend had chosen the drag name "Iona Traylor," she burbled that a friend of hers who'd worked at the Renaissance Festival had thought up a great name: "Master Bates!" Everyone blinked.

Here's another one: She heard me crack that Dallas (the rancher who turned out to be gay) was our Dairy Queen and so decided all of us needed meat and dairy nicknames. Cradling a bowl of chocolates in her ample (and usually inadequately contained) bosom, she became Swiss Miss. She thought I should be Rainbow Hamburger Buns. The other parties to the conversation moved on to another topic. Some minutes later she burst into violent, unsettling laughter.

"I know what Houston is!" she announced, referring to the rancher who bothered the cattle. "Sour cream!" Everyone blinked.

deity, I brought a six-pack of Belhaven Ale to the theater the next night.

He was by no means the most colorful of the men. The oldest had been a horn player in the surf band Dick Dale and the Delltones, and talked about Dale keeping a cheetah in his house and Toni Tenielle playing in Southern California hotel lounges. The youngest got the name "human satellite dish" for deft, quick-changing impersonations that flowed as effortlessly as his song parodies (featuring such crowd-pleasers as "Howlin' Out of Tune" and "Send in the Cows"). A third briefly captured our collective interest by announcing, broken-heartedly, that his girlfriend of eight years had made the "let's see other people" speech. Sympathy wavered when he explained that he'd been suspecting something was up and so in fact had already been seeing someone else, whom he had in fact already bedded. It evaporated when he made it clear that he was continuing with both women. The dominatrix later blamed this behavior for a migraine that had him moaning before curtain one night. ("All your blood is rushing to your penis!" she snapped.) "Are you offended by the fact that I'm sleeping with two women?" he asked. "It's none of our business," she countered, and that was exactly the point. The offense was not the action, but the telling.

Not-telling led to considerably longer-lasting intrigue around the actor cast as the moon-eyed poet, who was a dead ringer for Sheriff Woody in the animated film *Toy Story*. He didn't deny it when someone joked that one of the flower arrangements he received opening night was from his girlfriend and the other from his boyfriend. The music director, who attended a greater proportion of performances and parties than rehearsals,[43] began an obvious assault on the man at a cast party the next night, which sent

---

[43] And who Clueless didn't figure out was gay till this party, which caused her to repeat, "I knew he was anal, but I didn't know he was *that* anal!"

the "Is he, or isn't he?" speculation into high gear. Nobody cared about the answer, but if this nonsense was going to swirl about under our noses, we were not going to miss the opportunity to foment amusement.

Stolen from backstage between a Saturday matinee and a Friday call: one bandana (mine); one vacuum cleaner; one prop purse; the cast's stash of beer; the theater's entire supply of Hershey bars (for intermission sales), and hard candy (for a bowl in the lobby).

Soon enough, folks of all persuasion were falling under the spell of his big baby eyes. Crusty / Chesty / Busty Lou – whatever the hell her name was – was tossing a plastic cow at the boy, and gay audience members were privately confessing lust.[44] The only voice of discontent belonged to his on-stage partner, who chastised him for wooing her reluctantly. "You're the only person who has to kiss a girl and would you please act like you're enjoying it?" she lectured him. When speculation broke out in the communal dressing room as to why he hadn't shown up at yet another party, I suggested that when you have so many options it's hard to keep them straight – heh, heh. The sentiment was actually lost on two listeners, so I explained it, and ended up diving under the dressing table when he

---

[44] "Can we date him?" one man asked his lover. A cast member, whom I shall cloak with anonymity due to his/her being targeted in the denouement of this sordid little saga, explained the appeal: The man brought out the maternal instinct in women and the chicken hawk in men.

and Clueless walked in behind me midway. Far from being upset, the omni-directional lust target played right along, dropping his jeans offstage to show off leopard print boxer shorts and pronouncing that width meant more than length, "and I'm hung like a tuna can!"

A party at his apartment provided the opportunity to inspect for clues. Gracious, but definitely un-queeny (salsa with – pretzels?); décor dominated by display racks of souvenir golf balls, beer mugs, and, um, a set of longhorns…. Everything in sight argued against the growing hypothesis, which was furthered only by his own blatant invitations to look at his closet. After I left, one of the fomenters drew a red heart and puckered lips on the message board in his bedroom, around the name and number of the music director.

Two days later, in the last week of the run, our man of mystery sent me a vicious e-mail. It veered from incoherence to the very clear and serious charge of cattiness and ravaging his reputation. I was stunned. Had I really gone too far? Or had something been warped by a real-life version of Telephone and mis-attributed to me? Dreading the impact this outburst could have on the already tentative equilibrium of our tiny dressing room, I sent a response disavowing any ill intent and apologizing for any hurt.

I spoke too soon. Three other people (one completely uninvolved in the teasing) had received less coherent, but equally nasty mail. Two responded head-on before we all received the explanation: It was a joke! He'd generated hate mail from a website! He couldn't believe how sensitive we were! He was in stitches over our responses! And then he forwarded them, interlineated with spiteful, patronizing commentary. After which he invited me, cheerily, to meet him at a presentation for a multi-level marketing scheme.

Suddenly the sequel to *STEAK!* was not likely to be *POTATO!*, as previously speculated, but *BARBECUE!*, to be premiered when least suspected by the central character. At the very least, his pants were coming down in the saloon closing night.

In the meantime, dropping the subject seemed the safest course of action. By the next showtime he made it clear that this was not what he wanted. He scatter-shot ploys for attention, starting with spilling his guts in the dressing room over an incident at work that day. He'd received a request to cancel a long distance service calling card. Since it sounded like a college roommate who's always pulling pranks, he'd instructed the caller to cram it up his butt. Three times. Then he'd recognized the name from an order a year earlier. It really was a customer.

Within minutes of unloading his tale, he had told most of his unaffected cast members and asked everyone if they thought various people were mad at him. No one would get into it with him, and our collective off-handedness drove him nuts. He created an offstage tableau of despondency, sighing dramatically and burying his head in his lap. No one came near.

And thus closing night arrived, dripping with the promise of karmic reckoning. As with all things cosmic, the playing out veered from expectations. Our perpetrator's pants stayed on; much as she struggled, the saloonkeeper could not get his belt buckle undone, which was a shame because he wasn't wearing underwear. The foiled prank didn't go to waste, though. It careened into the next scene, which required him to ride around on a stick horse exclaiming that his prairie dog was popping up its little head when it didn't have any business doing that. "He's got a semi!" the saloonkeeper whispered from a peephole onto the stage. The refrain he sang throughout the scene, "gotta hold on," suddenly became "gotta hard on." As each of us entered, we rustlers took a look for ourselves. Sure enough, Woody's lookalike was sporting his namesake.

Dusty Lou was also on a public collision course. Her arch-conservative parents showed up to see exactly what their offspring had been up to all summer, even though she warned it would offend them. They didn't walk out, but her mother shot dirty looks, largely at me, for most of the show. Our youngster worked herself into a teary panic over how this was going to affect her parents' opinion of her (a worry that was, to my thinking, about two months too late). She went over the edge when Houston told her he'd put beer in the flask the three of us had to share. On top of everything else, the prospect of alcohol touching her virgin lips was too much for her. It wasn't beer, of course, but water, same as always, which splattered all over her face when she faked a swig. I complimented the prankster with a quote from astrologer Michael Lutin: "Mindfuck isn't a dirty word; it's a technical term for what men do to women."

Or, apparently, to anyone, as demonstrated by our sexually ambiguous cohort. And so it was on the dry ground of the Chisholm Trail that I met my first pirate of the High Seas. Avast, ye scurvy dog, indeed. Yeehaw!

How Can You Tell It's Performance Art?

Everyone's Wearing Black, and the Tickets Are Only Five Dollars

I thought it was dangerous performing in a theater with a ceiling that leaked onto the stage and flooded an unlit backstage passageway. That was before I scampered across the blade tip of the cutting edge known as Zocalo Theater and Performance Art Compound.

The Zocalo is a mélange of metal structures, some of which are art, actually enclosed, in a modest playground in a blue-collar enclave west of downtown Houston and south of the Heights. Though it's harder to find, the compound has a lot in common with the neighborhood's unofficial tourist attraction, a house that a retired railroad upholsterer covered with bits of beer cans. Each is a testament to an artist's vision – arguably warped, but undeniably tenacious – and ability to create something tangible out of refuse.

The Zocalo began as the studio, which is to say home, of a sculptor and performance artist named Nestor. He scrounged up enough seats and bare-bones equipment to turn one of the buildings into a workable theater. He threw the chain-link gates open long ago to the adventuresome and impecunious, some of whom have since taken up residence in unlikely, low-rent nooks and crannies of the compound, and some of whom just use the theater as a place to pretend that painting their faces white or dripping baked beans on themselves constitutes art. At some point this acquired

non-profit status, which has led to a governing structure that is inconsistent with the creator's unfettered reign.

What drew me into this personal injury suit waiting to happen was a parody of Thornton Wilder's *Our Town*, called *Not Our Town*. More accurately, the lure was the wheedling of the author/director, Joey Berner, the man (chronologically, at least) who'd directed *STEAK!* and talked nine other actors into joining the cast without seeing the script or being offered any specific part. One succumbed despite having been warned about the place. "Ever been to the Zocalo? No? You'll see," was the general gist. The timing of the production was a major point in its favor: Nestor had just left town to walk around the world for Art.

It's amazing that only one person ended up at the hospital, and that he wasn't one of us.

I thought I was on my way there the first time[45] one of the box fans sucked up my flowy black silk skirt. They provided the only ventilation, except for whatever wafted through the open doors. I would have predicted heat as the problem of working without air conditioning, in Houston, in summer (which lasts roughly till Thanksgiving), but that honor went to mosquitoes, whose breeding grounds were secreted somewhere on the property. Forget grease paint; our base was insect repellent (which bleached the dye on Danskin leotards, while leaving no marks on Target tights one-third the cost), fortified by a citronella candle that burned on-stage, even

---

[45] A deliberate phrasing that, yes, implies the existence of a subsequent time.

during performances.[46]

Tripping on things backstage was another constant. The Zocalo is a magnet for trash, that being the stuff from which it constantly recreates itself. It's a place where you could stumble on anything, even if it wasn't there a moment earlier. Every major pathway was lined with detritus from previous productions and projects – oversized animal costumes, chairs, ladders, boards, menacing tools, a coffin left over from *Woyzeck*. Every dash offstage was an exploration into the unknown, because unseen hands had a way of rearranging things during our absences – and once, behind our backs, when a can of white paint mysteriously upended and emptied itself directly in front of the dressing "room" (really a curtained hallway alongside the sole toilet) during the first act opening night.

People had a way of popping up unexpectedly, too. One night we arrived to a rehearsal in progress of Infernal Bridegroom Productions' *Guys & Dolls*, which wasn't even going to take place at the Zocalo. The resident in charge of theater use had given last-minute permission for the rehearsal, because, he said, he forgot about us. The competing director suggested it might stretch us artistically to rehearse for a change on the platform in front of the drive-in screen at one end of the parking lot. Since we were in the process of blocking which (to be of any use) required actually being in the intended space, Joey took the turn of events as an excuse to start drinking Shiner a couple of hours ahead of schedule. I was irked, but he

---

[46] At least our fire was in a container. The next production in the theater, the enigmatic *Eddie Goes to Poetry City*, which I would not recommend to any of you realists out there, had a set design that placed lit candles above a floor strewn with crumpled newspaper. After Eddie ignited a page and laid it on the concrete, I don't think anyone in the theater paid attention to anything he said or did until the paper burnt to ash. I certainly was braced for bolting at the first sign of a jumping spark.

wasn't, being more used to the ways of the Zocalo. He'd had to scuttle a rehearsal of an earlier production because a dog was chained to the stage.

Even when we had the stage to ourselves, we didn't, really. People were always wandering through rehearsals, which made some sense to me once I figured out that the only toilet (singular)[47] and shower (also singular) in the place were at the back of the theater. One repeat offender was a woman I recognized from odd places around town. Her behavior has always been mild and unthreatening, but something about her widened, vacant eyes and perpetual smile has always given me the creeps. Why doesn't she ever go home? I wondered. Because she was closer to it than we had any idea. On closing night someone got word that she was living above the dressing room. My stage husband and I inspected the allegation. Sure enough, in the rafters was a loft curtained with sheets.

But the real invasions began when Nestor resurfaced, way ahead of schedule. He made his presence known to us by locking the gate to the parking lot and losing the key, so we had to maneuver our cars into the unnervingly narrow corridor between the street and the adjoining, inexplicable, deep ditch. Since someone else had moved into what had been his house, he set up home in the school bus adjacent to his studio (as opposed to all the other buses on the lot). While we rehearsed, he went about his business, dragging heavy metal objects across the equally harsh surface of pavement, welding God knows what only feet away from actors running around the building to make an entrance, and taking showers. During the run, he began building a 30' tall armature for a monster pig that would figure in a Halloween fundraising event. It looked like a prop

---

[47] How singular was it? Poison ivy curled around the mirror, two hand-painted, misspelled signs threatened damnation to anyone who clogged the plumbing, and the wall between it and the dressing room blocked out only sights, not sounds.

from lost Fellini footage and turned the parking lot – which it consumed – into a tricky obstacle course requiring people directing traffic and double-parking up to five vehicles deep.

None of this, however, approached the marvels of closing night, when the spirit of Amok commandeered the theater and did its weird work. It arrived in the form of a truckload of drunks from Pasadena – not the home of the hot-rodding little old lady, but the land of oil refineries, putrid air, and bodies of water known to catch on fire. These people were friends and friends of friends of a cast member who had managed to alienate most of his colleagues just by existing. Over the course of the evening, I came to understand, and join, the consensus.

His pals, who had spent the day getting tanked at a street festival, caused trouble from the moment they showed up at the Zocalo an hour before curtain. As they pulled up, they tossed a beer can off the back of the truck onto the head of a person walking down the street, who happened to be a member of the cast. Most of them settled at the bar outside the theater, where they ambushed the rest of us on the way to the dressing room. A thin blonde with braces and a low-cut mini-dress that would have been sexy if she'd had any curves acted as gatekeeper, sticking her hand out, announcing, "Hi, my name is Rachel," and extracting a handshake from each of us as a sort of toll. Two of their brethren were already sitting in the theater, which had not been opened to the public. "Where's the nearest emergency room?" one of them asked me; he'd "busted" a kneecap while slam-dancing at the street festival and planned to go to the hospital – after the play.

Hi-my-name-is-Rachel threw up during the first act.

To her credit, she did it in the toilet, so that it was audible only to actors on the other side of the plywood wall in the dressing room. During intermission, she made herself known to large portions of the audience by sticking her hand at people and announcing, "Hi, my name is Rachel," as she butted in line for the restroom.

They were uncharacteristically quiet during the second act. Afterwards, they made up for it.

While the rest of us cleared out our gear and made tracks for a cast party, one big impediment to locking up the theater and leaving loomed at the bar. The driver of the truck had taken it, and the guy with the busted kneecap, to the hospital, and left the rest of the gang to wait at the Zocalo. "There's going to be bloodshed," the stage manager warned, urging me to flee to the cast party.

Things weren't less strange at the party. It was in a driveway, which had been filled with a coffee table, a lamp, a keg, a bunch of chairs, and a twin bed, onto which people were sprawling in ways that increasingly begged for privacy. The keg was well on its way to being tapped, and I recognized a few of the people who had been draining it. Like middle class grown-ups fleeing to the suburbs, cast members distanced ourselves from the noise and God knows what else by huddling at the edge of the sidewalk. We breathed a communal sigh of relief when Joey arrived with the news that he'd shooed the Pasadenans out of the Zocalo, locked the gates behind them, and left them standing in the street (there being no sidewalk, only concrete and, of course, ditches).

Not much later, a truck rounded the corner at break-neck speed. A

bunch of people were sitting in the bed, and one of them was standing, brandishing a sword, and hooting. They poured out of the vehicle like a thousand clowns and headed instinctively for the keg.

Over in suburbia, someone struck a match to light a cigar. The flame drew Hi-my-name-is-Rachel, who pushed her way into our circle to ask for a light for her cigarette. "I've never smoked a cigar," she admitted. "I guess that makes me a virgin." She pinched a waist into her cigarette and made it speak suggestively to men that were staring as glazed-eyed at the ground as I was. She soon returned to her people and the keg, and I retired down the street to do a long-promised card reading on the trunk of a car. The reading was interrupted by progress reports from an actor: Rachel was trying to show people her belly button. Rachel was lifting her dress. Rachel was creating a difference of opinion among witnesses; one camp thought she was wearing a thong, while the other swore she wasn't wearing underwear.

The potential for danger was escalating, as well as the noise level. Sure it was only a matter of time until the police arrived, several of us suburbanites decided to hike to a Mexican restaurant for breakfast. We returned an hour later to an absolutely vacant driveway, which had been cleared, we learned later, voluntarily and not under threat of police action. Amok had one last trick: removing my keys from my purse. My companions dwindled to one as we pondered what to do about the situation. The light was on in our host's bathroom. I banged and banged on his door to no avail, then put my hand in my hand and touched: my keys.

Pages from a Stage Manager's Notebook

What Can Go Wrong?

Lots, actually. Experience teaches that the one thing that you don't prepare for will be the one thing that goes haywire. That has informed my career in event production; herewith proof of this Rule of Life.

For Example, This

There are storm clouds early on the day of the Gay Men's Chorus of Houston's premiere concert in the Wortham Center (home to Houston Grand Opera), which features five other choruses from around the state. I'm there as stage manager and token straight woman; the entire technical crew is union, male, and increasingly hell bent on proving just how straight-arrowedly-red-blooded they are.

The crew, except for the sound guy, spends the three-hour tech check either on the loading dock eating an extended lunch, or being invisible. When we corner the light guy because he has not set up half of the lighting, he makes it clear that he has not read the cue sheet and doesn't intend to, ever, even during the concert; he'll just look out from the booth and adjust the lights to look "nice." The stage crew tells me they prefer not to wear headsets, so I shouldn't rely on being able to talk to them during the show, but should give a curtain signal with a red warning light. I ditch any thought of merely calling the cues and decided to specify every technical move in intelligence-insulting detail.

The opening number goes without a hitch. Ensembles sing, angel-like, from the top of the balcony, the back of the sold-out house, and the wings, process down the aisles, and assemble on stage; by the end, a burst of emotion jumps palpably from the 250 or so singers to the 1000+ audience members, who go berserk with applause. I hit the signal to lower the curtain. Nothing moves. I hit the button again and again. The applause is dying down; the singers are beginning to look confused. I look to the far wing and see: no one. It dawns on me that the stage crew has left the stage. I dispatch my assistant to find them; I'm making inquiries over the headset as to their whereabouts, all the while waving and mouthing "Get off the stage!! Get off!" at the bewildered performers. They begin to move like distracted cattle; the curtain

comes down (my assistant broke union rules – *oooooo!* – and lowered it his non-card-carrying self); I broadcast even-toned instructions over the P.A. for Jack and Hank to return to the stage because our program calls for the curtain to be repeatedly raised and lowered during the first act.

"We apologize," a voice says through the headset a few minutes later. "We misread the cue sheet." Yeah, right, like "Cue 3: Curtain down" is ambiguous. My spoken response, heard by most of the chorus over the backstage monitors, passes into legend well before intermission. What leaves my lips escapes my memory; Rex repeats it back to me as a terse "Apology noted." Somehow, my refusal to take the time to rip these guys to shreds only increases my cachet among several hundred revenge-thirsty queens, two of whom will later take it upon themselves to provide my fill of gin and tonic. "Good thing you're not a prosecutor!" Rex exclaims, marveling at my perceived cold-bloodedness. From my end it feels like an advanced case of being stunned.

And what has the errant crew been doing? Moving large bits of lumber about in elevators and underground corridors – directly into the path of throngs of choristers trying to get back to their dressing rooms. The hall's technical director will deem the mishap the worst in the building's history and dock the evening pay of the stage and light crew. Once off the job, I finally name the tune that's been playing off in the distance. Sounds suspiciously like homophobia to me.

And Then There's This

Jesus showed up backstage after the technical setup for the Gay Men's Chorus of Houston 15th Anniversary Concert and tried to baptize us, so we had to throw him out.

None of us recognized him as such at first. He was bigger and more animated than the last time I saw him (when he was still in his molded plastic crèche form). This time he appeared in the guise of one of the chorus members, and soaking wet at that. He approached a group of us in the wings (including, conveniently, a psychiatric nurse) and asked for a towel. When we had none to offer, he took a seat and advised us of the following:

He was leaving for Washington after the concert, even if he had to go on foot; the evening's concert was dedicated to him; all his life he has had special powers, which God had now activated to carry out the mission for which he had been sent to this planet; he had in fact become God and, as such, was now going to bless us; and we could (a) let him bless us, (b) feel sorry for him, or (c) throw him out.

He stood up, dipped one hand in a Styrofoam cup he was clutching and, in a failure of divine wisdom, chose as first recipient the biggest and tallest of us, who simply and gently stopped the moistened hand. Our would-be savior turned on his heel and squished his way out of the building. Since this incident was the most over-the-edge in a recent escalation of danger signals, it didn't take much urging from the psych nurse for the biggest and tallest of us to instruct the stage door security guard not to let the man backstage again. The guard said she'd have no trouble recognizing him, because she'd seen him several times over the last month – walking in a fountain downtown.

Wherever You Go, There You Are

Someone's Knocking at the Door

The unmistakable smell of gas in the apartment late one evening sounded the alarm for two phone calls: one reporting the leak to the gas company, and one seeking a human buffer against the prospect of an Entex employee, presumably male, working into the night in the home of a single woman. Rex Protector was too bogged down with work to send his body over, but he did agree to inject his being into the situation via a schedule of calls in each direction. We needn't have worried. Within 30 minutes, two Entex employees, both demonstrably male, drove up in a big truck with dramatically circling lights. Tony, who looked like a Hispanic Lou Costello, performed the work of actually locating the leak and replacing the pipe. Tim, who looked and talked like an Anglicized variant of the same, performed the work of holding a clipboard, looking over his companion's shoulder, and poking around a stranger's living room.

"You got a Ouija board," he announced, looking at a knockoff board (Mystic Prophet) atop a framed poster.

"It's an old one," I explained; a friend had passed it on when he was clearing out his childhood home.

This information impressed Tim. "That could be worth a lot of money," he deduced, "But I don't mess with Ouija boards." He moved back to the furnace door to hover over his companion.

"I don't either," I assured him, "Not since one called me a bitch when I was in high school."

This struck Tim and Tony as hysterical. It also set Tim thinking.

"You know, there's a lot of stuff they don't tell us," Tim said, sliding his back down the doorway into a squat. What the "stuff" had to do with was UFOs, largely. "There's got to be more out there than they're telling us," he insisted, then added by way of example, "The Milky Way is a needle in a haystack."[48] This is something he knows quite a bit about because he used to read a lot of science fiction. Doesn't anymore, though; reading that stuff made him wonder about noises around the house. "You ever do that?"

"That's why I don't go to creepy movies," I confessed. "They get under my skin and I can't get to sleep at night."

He wandered back into the living room. "You got old books up there. Mind if I look at them? I won't touch them," he assured me.

"Go right ahead," I said. "The leather binding is cracking, so if you pick one up, it'll crumble and your hands will get all red."

He peered up at them respectfully. "What are they?" he asked, walking back to his command post in the doorway. I explained that they're German encyclopedias from the late 1800s. Tim whooshed through a rollercoaster

---

[48] The importance of this statement didn't hit me till I related the evening's events to Rex. What had lured me out of the apartment while the leak was springing was a speech in the Inprint Writers' Business Series. The first speaker, who is a published and even acclaimed novelist, walked on stage in long, deep purple swallowtails, a bow tie of like color, a tuxedo shirt, and a green fright wig, with whiteface and big red hearts drawn on her cheeks. She made the experience even more memorable by punctuating her speech, at appropriate moments, with dead-on impersonations of Betty Boop ("I wanna be loved by you, just you..." on through "boop-boop-ba-doop"), Billie Holliday (a verse of "Ain't Nobody's Business If I Do"), and Marlene Dietrich ("I can't giff you anything but luff, baby"). She asked questions of the audience, and whenever someone answered a question correctly (effectively, any time anyone bothered to offer an answer), she would fling a candy bar at them. Not exactly to them; she suffers the muscle memorization deficiency that plagues so many of us whose inherent girlness kept us, for one reason or another, from being taught how to pitch. What's important here is not how efficiently they reached their intended destinations, but the label on these airborne offerings: Milky Way.

of subjects – describing the hyperactive old man landlord at the last place they had to repair, venturing a correct guess that mine is snoopy, then pointing out how badly Tony's cat had scratched up his hands when he tried to put it in a pet taxi. Tony showed me the location of the main valve for the gas line; I had only turned off the valves directly into the furnace. They were amazed to hear I had been the person who'd lit the pilot in the first place. "You did that yourself?" Tim asked. "Sure, it's easy," I said, "And besides, doing it myself keeps my landlord out of my place."

He responded, "I made sure my sister learned how to change a tire." I took note of the leap in logic and threw it back at him. "Hey, I know guys who won't light their own pilot because they're afraid they'll blow up." Both T-men laughed. Then it was time for another stroll around the room. (It sounds like he was casing the place, Rex commented later, but possessed sufficient ineptitude to constitute a real threat.)

"Are these collectibles?" he asked, the floor-to-ceiling shelves of toys having caught his eye. "It's a wind-up toy collection," I explained. "Wow, look, the Beatles!" he said to his partner, who continued prosecuting the purpose of their visit. Tony met his goal first. On the way out, Tim pointed out my record albums to his partner. "Look at all those from the sixties!" he exclaimed; I never saw him get close enough to be able to read the spines. Tony jumped into the conversation with a smile. "Bet you've got Iron Butterfly in there!" he grinned. "No," I said, walking them out the door, "I don't have 'In-a-gadda-da-vida.'" "I do!" Tony exclaimed. "When I want to get back at my neighbors I crank it up!" They bounded into the night, leaving the echo of "See you later" in their wake, with time to spare before the appointed check-up call from Rex.

Blood Curse

They say that what you're doing at midnight on New Year's Eve sets the tone for the next 12 months. Once, when the witching hour between years arrived, I was with five gay men, one of whom lingered at my side till 5:30 a.m. (The only other male to stay up all night with me was my high school boyfriend, who decided in college to cast his lot for the other side of the fence.)

The next New Year's Eve brought three invitations and a desire to socialize that overpowered a relapse of agonizing throat and ear pain that should have debilitated any sensible person. I approached the invitations in the order of their arrival. At T-minus 20, I realized that the only men who were talking to me, at a well- and largely-hetero-populated affair, were gay. Damned if I was going to ring in another year shoulder to shoulder pad with a gay man. I took a hint from the growing aching to make a quiet exit.

The route home took me by the site of invitation #2, so I stopped by in time for champagne at midnight, in the highly acceptable midst of writers, slackers, and computer programmers. Not long into the new year, a nearby conversation group yelled at me to come on over and join their lawyer bashing. One of the bashers turned out to be someone from my law school class, whom I hadn't seen for 13 years. When we started trading tales of disillusionment, the rest of the group disbanded in disgust – except for one man, whose comments revealed escalating intimate knowledge of the lawyer. Oh, no. Oh, yes. Before he let slip a reflexive use of "old married couple," I knew. I heard the exit cue and went home. Alone.

The damned thing about adages is that they're true. You can run, but you can't hide. At least, I can't.

Well, Shiver Me Timbers

One thing about the High Seas: you never know when a tsunami'll swell up and knock you over on dry land.

I had to have a probate court appoint an appraiser for some old houses owned by an estate. The appointee turned out to be a judge, whose office referred me to an employee in the county appraisal office, who turned out to be an aging woman with an emphysemic voice. "All of Montrose is run down," she scoffed on hearing the houses' location. When she asked if it's possible to get into the houses, I warned that she'd have to pick the keys up from a kind of weird location. "How weird?" she asked cautiously. "A leather shop," I answered; the shop's owner is a family friend who has been managing the properties. "Oh, goodie," she barked. "I'll have to bring along a girlfriend. This could be fun!"

Before I could close the conversation, she added that she and a man, never identified beyond the name Tony, had once gone to Montrose for a masturbation workshop. "We saw a bag man on the street and Tony was worried that I thought he was coming after me. I said, 'Tony, in this neighborhood, I think it's you he's after!'"

She expedited my work.

Son of a...

My final stint of volunteering at the annual Orange Show benefit served up the usual incomparable moments of brushing up against unfathomable wealth. The event took place in October, in the enormous sculpture garden of an enormous River Oaks estate. Some of the installations were so remarkable that a security guard assumed the mantle of tour guide and kept pointing them out to us plebeian volunteers. He was particularly taken with a gargantuan replica of a nail, while I was entranced by an art nouveau arch that had once marked the entrance to a Paris subway station. An actor acquaintance had been entrusted with a golf cart, which he had appropriated for giving tours of the grounds. I got a long bumpy one, dashing through trees and circling that unavoidable nail, and a second, more direct tour at the end of my stay. The driver offered a ride back to my car, with the added indulgence of delivering the cart to the side of the outdoor stage, right behind the car waiting for the performer, where I was enjoying a close-range profile view of Chuck Berry's half-hearted act.

What made the evening, though, were not these vignettes, nor rumors of decadently luxurious bathrooms, nor recurring glimpses of wizened, excessively orange Billy Gibbons shuffling through the proceedings. The high point came while I was actually engaged in the reason for my being there in the first place. Two high school-aged girls in alarmingly expensive cocktail attire asked for Tarot readings about men. Their choice of word got my attention, given that they didn't look older than juniors. Sure enough, a man, and not a boy, showed up in the spread of one of them. She explained that she had a crush on her older brother's friend. "He lives in Austin," she said. "He's the son of a Bee Gee."

Go ahead; say it out loud. I did. This one's bound to be useful for something. Son of a Bee Gee!

'Tis the
Season

A Christmas Memory

Cold weather sent memories of making fruitcake to Truman Capote; "Winter Wonderland" unleashes a more demonic recall on my part. What set this off for me lately was a rehearsal for a holiday cabaret, the cast of which includes my friend John and me. The men's number, "Walking 'Round in Women's Underwear," parodies my trigger song and involves minueting, voguing, and chorus-line kicking while singing about lacy silk things.[49] In one of the early run-throughs, the movements disintegrated

---

[49] It will be a revelation how this rendition will go over at this theater, on the most white-bread outskirts of Houston, which draws a superannuated core audience that has as much difficulty physically maneuvering into the seats as it does getting the point of much of the programming. At the end of Ibsen's *A Doll's House*, when the completely sheltered Nora walked out on her loutish husband, Western literature cracked open, never to be the same; but when the lights went up on the performance I saw at this theater, the seventyish woman at the other end of the front row barked in a stage whisper, "Naughty ending!"

The verdict? The prancing was no problem for those who didn't walk out when Gabriel showed what really happened that first Christmas (complete with a probably-historically-accurate uncomfortably pregnant, black Mary).

into widespread stumbling. The director, sitting in the audience, threw his hands up and shouted like a shaky Jewish patriarch, "My people! My people! What's happened to my people?" The men's defense: while they may all be queens, none has ever been a *drag* queen.

When the laughter died down, what surfaced in me was a 25-year-old parody of the same song. I was the author, and I'd been memorializing something that had erupted backstage during a production of *Fiddler on the Roof*. (Ah, the lattice of coincidences hovers again. Things theatrical and Jewish. What does it all mean?) (Nothing!) My vantage point was the light booth, where I was working a follow spot, which is to say that I did not actually experience the story I put into song. But it hit my ears within minutes of occurring, because a witness ran into the booth during intermission screaming a most attention-getting news flash: "Nelson's trying to kill Bill!" Nelson was the head of the heaven crew, a senior more full of himself than most, with an early Dartmouth admission in hand. Bill, a junior, was the backstage member of the lighting crew, whose duties positioned him several feet below Nelson's post on the catwalk. Bill heard Nelson ask to have a board tossed up to him; Nelson screamed that Bill had thrown the board at him; and the only fact not in dispute was that Nelson had scrambled down the ladder onto the stage and had Bill in a choke hold.

My first attempt to process a friend's near-death through writing took the form of a revenge fantasy:

Nelson roasting on an open wire,
Hot blood dripping on your toes

No further lines coming on this theme, I turned to immortalizing the incident. This approach succeeded, or at least ran to completion. I give you now what was running through my head when four gay men were tripping over themselves on stage.

Nelson screams, "I will kill you!"
Susan cries as he tries to
Strangle poor Bill,
Give him a thrill,
Chill him with the power of his hands.

In the heaven you can find a person
Who believes that he's Almighty God
He'll say, "Toss me that board,"
You'll say, "No, sir!"
'Cause if you throw it
He'll come running down

From the heaven to kill you
And he won't stop till you're blue,
A nervous wreck,
Frightened like heck,
Strangled by the power of his hands.

Real-Life Magic
Featuring St. Nick

Three stories in honor of St. Nicholas Day

L ate one evening I was zigzagging a path across a well-populated sidewalk in the Indian section of Jackson Heights, Queens. My destination was the subway station, but movement in a shop window made me stop. In the window of a CD store was a mechanical figure swinging its hips back and forth. It had big black boots with enormous buckles, rosy cheeks, and a thick white beard and hair. A torn piece of muslin was wrapped around its frame in a sort of sarong, and another piece formed a cap like a knotted spiral. It was Santa Sikh! A smile stayed with me to the end of the block.

A friend and her daughter used to celebrate this holiday in the heart of Texas, but with a twist: They'd assemble packages for the girl's playmates and go out the night of December 5 to leave them on doorsteps. A few years back, while they were making their preparations, the girl started gloating about how funny it was that her girlfriends think that St. Nicholas visits them only he doesn't; it's really her and her mom. "But the real one visits me!" she announced, radiantly.

Even more years back, my family took a stab at celebrating St. Nicholas Day ourselves. We were living in Munich, where my dad was on sabbatical, and had the middle floor in a three-family house. Early in the evening, my mother pulled off some approximation of a visit from the saint himself, which involved depositing a bag at the door and tricking us into finding

it. I'm sure it had candy, and I'm sure we'd ripped into it and long since put it aside by the time the knock came.

Or maybe it was the interior doorbell; I can't be sure. What I do know for certain was that it was not the outside doorbell, which you had to ring to be let into the gate and then the front door of the house. This came from the hallway just outside our door.

I went to the door and opened it. On the landing was a man in a red bishop's outfit, wearing an enormous oval hat and carrying a crook. He said he was St. Nicholas, and said it in English. I asked him to wait, ran to the bathroom, and started yelling at my mother, who was behind the door in the bath: "MOM! ST NICHOLAS IS HERE!"

The next thing I remember is the sight of him in the dining room, which was crammed with dark, ornately carved cabinetry covered with demonic, pointy-tongued heads. He was slowly, solemnly proclaiming in pretty decent English that our names were in his book of good children. He opened a huge book and showed us, and damned if there wasn't an entry for the Biehl children. He gave us a bag of fruit and nuts and took his leave. Our jaws were still hanging. The landlady's little girl ran out of their downstairs apartment and looked down the street after him.

Our landlady told us that he was a university student who'd been hired by families in the neighborhood to pay a visit to their children. Somebody had gone to the trouble — I'm guessing she was the culprit — to include the pack of American kids on the second floor.

The Perils of Professional Christmas Caroling

hristmas caroling for pay is like working at an amusement theme park that's delivered on site and on demand. You become a piece of the vast machinery of Christmas, the entertainers and costumes and props that create the backdrop against which other people experience nostalgia and joy and, more often than not, boredom.

Your particular gear is likely to be stuck in the Victorian age, or someone's misperception of it. Odds are you're dressed for a bitter cold that exists only in your employer's imagination, which at least allows laughably wide latitude in the historical accuracy of your clothes.[50]

You work in situations Dickens could have never imagined. No matter how absurd, you do what you're told, whether it's keeping company with taxidermied emus alongside an indoor pool, or singing the most religious of carols next to an eyeglass cleaning machine belching steam in a flea market.

---

[50] I felt a strange kinship with a sparkling red package I spied at one gig in a street near the curb. A tear in the wrapping revealed the contents: a brick.

Sometimes you are an annoyance, others the object of unexpected adoration. Most of the time, you are invisible. But always, you are just part of the hired help, staying out of the way until bidden. You share an unspoken camaraderie with other threads in the holiday fabric, particularly hard-working ones like waiters, who can also, not incidentally, hand you goodies. You disavow any relationship with certain others that can bring only irritation, that are dressed even more ridiculously than you, that are the occupational hazard of the party circuit, that are, and I shudder at even writing the word, clowns.

Judge not in haste; consider first this tenet of clown behavior: A clown is never off stage. He will impose his antics no matter what, even if you are not part of the audience for which he was hired, and even while on break. In his gloved hands, the Protestant work ethic becomes a tool of sadism.

Harsh words, but true, the harvest of exasperating experience. Prejudice can grow from only one bad apple, and I met mine at a private dining club. It was the beginning of an eight-hour job. We carolers were taking our places by the elevators when one of the doors opened. Out stepped a clown we recognized from the previous year, who'd sullied the lunch break by telling joke after joke that had fallen flat. He waved. We waved. He walked by, and the noise started.

Squeak. Squeak. Squeak. "He's squeaking," I said. It didn't stop. Squeak. Squeak. Squeak. The source of the noise wasn't his monstrously oversized shoes. It was his hands. His very hands held the promise of a day of tiresome encounters. After the squeaking faded down the long hallway and around the corner, I hinted at the possibility of committing murder before the day was over. "I heard that!" he yelled. "I'll say it to your face!" I yelled back.

We had to sit in a room with this man to eat lunch. We didn't sing at the table. Santa didn't ho-ho-ho. But the clown was compelled to hit his knife against a water glass and announce, "A toast! To bread. Because without bread, there could be no toast." Which is exactly what he had said the year before.

We singers gulped down lunch and fled to the outdoors, where we spent the rest of the break promenading along the sidewalks of downtown Houston in fake Victorian finery and 80-degree heat, singing Broadway show tunes and fielding inquiries from horse-drawn carriage drivers about where our men had purchased their capes.

Back in the lobby, the clown had news for us. "I've brought reinforcements," he announced, as a blue-haired creature pushed a box on wheels past us. This clown was even worse. It had a voice that generally only results from sucking helium. Christmas may have been only seven days away, but it felt like forever.

The Center Cannot Hold

It Was Supposed to Be A Return to Love

It Turned Into a Descent to Hell

One of my new year's resolutions was linking up with a New York literary agent. It happened in 21 days, when one actually phoned with the request that I organize a speech in March for a client on a book tour – Marianne Williamson, who'd written an extended essay on *A Course in Miracles* called *A Return To Love*. The event was pitched as extremely low-key; it was slated for a Sunday evening at the 250-seat sanctuary of First Unitarian Universalist Church of Houston, where I have been singing for eight years, and would require only a couple of people to work the door. I repeated back the list of duties (a policy of mine, since people have a way of expanding them once I agree to an involvement) and was assured it was all. My name and phone number would be omitted from all publicity, all of which would be directed to the bookstore handling the speech. They agreed to my fee.

Ominous music: swell up and out.

The first little wrinkle came with the announcement that Marianne was going on *The Oprah Winfrey Show*, whose host considered this the most important book since Scott Peck's *The Road Not Taken*, and had allegedly bought 1000 copies. Would there be another, larger hall where the speech might take place? Could I see my way to making a few calls? I sought out a number of places and zeroed in on the sanctuaries of Emerson Unitarian

CONFESSIONS OF A THIRD-RATE GODDESS

Church and Unity, the pyramid-shaped structure that people are always confusing with my denomination. Even though Marianne Williamson is a Unity author, the Houston church staff was doubtful that its xenophobic doors would be opened even for her. After submitting the matter to the special projects committee, the secretary called back to pass on a few questions from the committee, then stopped herself. "What am I doing?" she said. "We have services on Sunday night." This precluded using Unity and I made arrangements, not without some finagling and relying heavily on my connection with First Unitarian, to rent the Emerson sanctuary. (By the by, Emerson is the "family" congregation, which has been known to refer women in pantsuits to the "downtown" congregation, 1st U., which employs a gay Zen Buddhist minister and, as its director of religious education, a practicing witch.)

The next week, the *Oprah* segment aired and the first printing sold out.

I started getting phone messages from the Unity minister himself. Turned out that, what do you know, the church doesn't have services on Sunday nights; he had no idea why the secretary might have told me that, and he'd love to work with me to get the speech at Unity. I set out the only way the switch could be made: The church would have to let me bring in an outside bookstore to sell Marianne's books. The rest of the week was interrupted by a barrage of phone calls from various Unity personnel posing the same question and hearing – but not listening to – the same response. The most frequent was the Unity bookstore manager, who kept saying, "What can you do for us?" and finally, on the day before the publisher's publicity was going to the printer, acted on the suggestion to discuss the matter directly with the owner of Body Mind & Soul Books, which had already ordered several hundred copies in anticipation of the event. Somewhere in the conversation, the Unity store manager finally understood that this speech was part of a *book tour*, which she reported

as if it were news to me in the final phone call retracting Unity's offer to shelter the event.

I mentioned to the agent that my services were going considerably beyond what we had agreed and maybe he should adjust the percentage. Coincidentally or not, he put me on hold.

Several Sundays later, an advance piece appeared in a paper. The next day, a bedraggled staffer phoned to whine – as best as a person can who's losing her voice – that Body Mind & Soul had fielded several hundred calls that Sunday and could they please sell advance tickets. The word from New York was immovable: Marianne had "an issue" with advance sales. Calls begging for reservations deluged the bookstore, the church, the supposedly anonymous organizer's law office (i.e., mine), and even my home answering machine. The most unnerving was an out-of-state caller who said she'd gotten my name and phone number in a holy encounter. The prospect of Messianic New Agers channeling information about me was not out of the realm of possibility. When another caller cited the same source a few days later, I was relieved to learn that "A Holy Encounter" was a *Course In Miracles* newsletter from California.

The actual event spun out of control, despite all efforts to rein it in. I've weathered 11th-hour near-litigation brawls involving sound system problems and performers' sexual preferences, dealt with a collapsing piano, and juggled the codependent needs of 200+ radical feminists, but never in my event production experience had I ever encountered the problem that downed me 30 minutes before speech time, when my eyesight, hearing and, eventually, sense of balance dimmed. After a brief knee-clutching (and body-cursing) break, I returned to the helm of what was growing into self-replicating protoplasm. Due to a misperception of the number of tickets in a roll – 1000 instead of 500 – a planned method of keeping tabs on seat count fell apart completely, which I was stunned to learn when the president of the congregation ran out of the sanctuary yelling that I had to shut down the door and I walked into a room overflowing with people in the aisles, along the walls, in the window sills, in the choir loft, and on the floor along the altar and the podium. Despite such dangerous overcrowding, late-comers still fought being turned away with a disturbing pattern of anguished moaning about how far they'd driven and how desperately they had to see Marianne. The restrooms ran out of toilet paper before the speech started.

The actual speech was lost on the organizer (i.e., me), who, when not crouching on a floor battling an adding machine to reconcile the take (which yielded a percentage that left me more than happy), spent the time cowering over exactly what horrid fate Authority was going to impose for the overcrowding. Under the watchful eye of the congregation's president, whose very presence was making me feel more and more in trouble, my dwindling crew broke down the set-up with 10 minutes to spare before the end of the rental.

When I returned the key to the office the next morning, I saw the congregation president walking on the grounds and tried to will myself into invisibility. I failed. He called me over to introduce me to his companion, who turned out to be Emerson's minister. I braced for the worst, and both men surprised me– the president by praising my organizational abilities, and the minister by laughing that the next time, I should use the George

R. Brown Convention Center.

Postscript 27 years later: I did briefly meet Marianne before the event, at a 5-star hotel near the Houston Galleria. She was holding an infant and barely noted my presence, a reaction presaging a lack of any acknowledgment of my effort the evening of the event.

The bookstore owner, on the other hand, thanked me repeatedly for not screwing her over by going with Unity and sticking her with hundreds of books. Never occurred to me to do that.

The Monkey's Paw, Revisited

I got a book contract. Champagne flowed; celebrations ensued; every writer's dream was coming true.

It was a dream, all right. Here are a few highlights:

The acquisitions editor (AE) gave me four days to prepare a proposal for a *Netscape Guide to Legal Research*, which I'd never thought of writing till she first called me a few weeks earlier. I did it.

By the time the contract arrived, overnighted an inexplicable two weeks after my co-author (whose name I will not drag into this stupid, sordid saga because she did not cause, nor deserve, any of it) had signed it at the publisher's offices – only two weeks were left, by its terms, to turn in 25% of the manuscript. I got an extension, which AE blithely declined to put in writing. I also got the writers' guidelines and learned that, while scrambling to get the first installment of the manuscript completed on the truncated timeline, I had to use Microsoft Word. This meant I had to buy and learn Microsoft Word, which I did not own, being a lawyer and by definition a WordPerfect user.[51] I did it.

A week before the first deadline, I learned that, contrary to the writers' guidelines, the screenshots I had to turn in along with the chapters had to use a version of Windows I did not own. While scrambling to meet

---

[51] I see no amusing coincidence in Microsoft's choice of music for its commercials being Mozart's "Confutatis Maledictis" ("The damned and the accursed are convicted to flames of hell"). Its software is demonic, wasting our time to the point of wasting our lives.

the truncated deadline, I had to buy and learn a new operating system, which also meant buying and installing a new hard drive, not to mention upgrading all my critical applications. I did it.[52]

Before the 50% deadline, the development editor quit.

Then the AE let me know that a deal was in the works to associate the book with a Major National Internet Service Provider, so all the screenshots were going to have to be redone using its interface. Since I do not use this MNISP and refused to change one more aspect of my computer set-up, she assured me that the publisher would take care of the screenshots.

The AE quit. So did the person responsible for processing invoices.

The day before the 100% deadline, the head of acquisitions told me that the MNISP's lawyers were dragging their feet, but he was sure the deal was going through so the book's browser affiliation was being switched to Internet Explorer – and I would to have to rewrite every browser reference in the manuscript, which meant I was going to have to figure out Internet Explorer, which I don't use. The restructuring he'd come up with behind our backs also meant throwing out three of the chapters I'd just finished, and expanding my co-author's obligations from one chapter to three. We did it.

---

[52] Swearing every step of the way. My friend Ben, who heroically installed the hard drive, observed much of it, since he sat by as moral support while I installed the new operating system. He laughed while I cursed – at each screen prompt, at each status report, even at the twinkling band of colors at the bottom of the Windows 95 boot-up screen, which annoyed me with their gleeful gobbling of precious system resources. The time came to launch the system. I hesitated and looked at Ben before carefully pressing "Start." As my finger hit the key, the radio burst out with Mick Jagger singing, "Start me up." The swearing gave way to hysterical laughter. A few days later Ben e-mailed a more appropriate alternative to that tune: a Jagger sound clip again, this time singing, "Pleased to meet you; hope you guessed my name." *See n.51 above.*

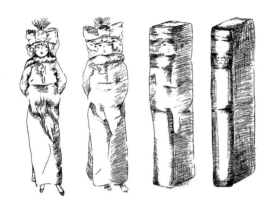

After six weeks or so of my submitting and re-submitting an invoice, and receiving repeated reassurances that it had been / was being / would be processed, and getting the new AE to swoop down on these people like a banshee, a check was finally overnighted as promised. To the wrong address. Where someone signed for it. Before the publisher stopped payment on the check and started the whole rigmarole again, the recipient responded to my woeful typewritten plea and handed over the envelope, unopened.

Rumors surfaced that the publisher wasn't going to survive a merger at the end of the year. Imagine my surprise.

All of the chapters came back at once from technical and copy editing for final author review, about a month after I'd been told to expect them, and in the thick of major work obligations I'd postponed to this time just so they wouldn't conflict with the book. The project editor asked when they could expect the re-done screenshots. I reminded her I wasn't doing them. Well, the intern who was going to do them wasn't there anymore, so they were my problem. Oh, yeah? I invoked my guardian banshee, who emailed that she would fly to Texas and break my arms if I agreed to do them. I didn't.

Rumors were confirmed.

The week the book went into production, the project editor was called out of town to a conference. Her replacement and I still got the galleys proofed before press date. Silence ensued. The publication date came and went. More silence.

More than three months later, the publisher's new owner canceled the book and asked me to pay the advance back. I didn't.

What doesn't kill me makes me stronger. And glad I'm a lawyer.

I Walked Through the Valley of Death and Lo, I Feared Not

But I Was Mighty Dazed

This year, deaths and sudden endings erupted around me like popcorn kernels heating in a covered pan. There was hardly time to experience one development, much less process it, before the next came down my phone line, landed on my doorstep, or walked into my office.

While the tsunami of mortality (as a distant observer dubbed it) was cresting, it exceeded the emotional capacity of long-term confidants who've seen plenty in a decade of proximity to Ground Zero of weird. People who came into more casual contact simply listened till their coping mechanisms gave out, at which point they usually blurted, "This doesn't sound real!"

In retrospect, the catalog of events still strains credulity. In the first wave alone, which lasted slightly more than two weeks, one friend and one client died, I attended both funerals, my favorite aunt had a transient stroke, I brushed my finger against a meat cleaver in a kitchen drawer and ended up in an ER for five stitches, my then boyfriend's father entered the same ER with what turned out to be a warning stroke, his brother fainted in the shower the next day and was taken to a different ER, and their father had, and survived, arterial surgery.

In the brief lull that followed, I saw a play that turned out to be not much of a diversion. *Marisol* begins with the namesake character making

it home from work and into bed alive only through the repeated intervention of her guardian angel. Her protector materializes to warn that God is dying and taking the world with Him, so all the angels are throwing down their wings to go to war against Him, which will make the world unrecognizable. Soon enough, cow's milk turns salty, men give birth, snow falls in 100+ degree weather, the sun sets in the north, Neo-Nazis set fire to the homeless.

This is not too far off from reality, I thought.

Then the gloves came off. March began with a voice mail message that my high school choir director had been found bludgeoned to death in his home. This was not news to be noted with a platitude and then brushed aside. He had made the most profound impact of any teacher on the course of my life, because he had somehow talked my fiscally conservative parents into letting me take voice lessons. The news prompted a flurry of phone calls and letters reconnecting classmates who'd been out of touch for years. No one knew any details, but everyone had an awe-filled story about the influence he'd wielded.

Since the memorial service was 200 miles away, and on a weeknight, I decided to participate long-distance by burning a candle and listening to a recording. Minutes before the service started, my closest girlfriend said she had just been diagnosed HIV+. The choir track of choice, a Brahms motet ("Wherefore have the light been granted to the weary of spirit?") took on a meaning that had escaped my adolescent self. Within a week, another friend's lungs collapsed. Then my brother unloaded the revelation that his wife of 16 years had been meeting men online.

I'd been braced for the second; years of AIDS-related problems had been wearing down my mystic friend David, who'd stayed close even after moving from Houston to Seattle. The bookend news items, though, were out of the blue. Any one of the three developments alone would have been devastating; each involved a refuge from an illogical, battering, competitive world (my brother's marriage especially serving as welcome DMZ), an unfailing source of support of all kinds, a relationship so special that labels are inadequate and ultimately belittling. All three teetering at once was unthinkable, so I refused to dwell on the inevitable ramifications. I faced only what the moment presented.

Focusing on what could be done, however little, worked as a coping mechanism. Most of the time, that amounted only to listening, especially in the cases of David and my brother. For my girlfriend, though, I tried to ferret out resources, and help, and information. The bookmarks on my web browser swelled in a new and distasteful direction; a slew of leads on medical information and local resources joined the *X-Files* and *Star Trek* pages I'd already found for her.

I Know a Secret

Without revealing her identity, I asked a male friend who is HIV+ to breakfast to help prepare for what might lie ahead psychologically. No slouch in the intuition department himself, he figured out who I was talking about and burst into tears in the restaurant. Because of her job as an elementary school social worker, and her own fundamental sense of privacy, she was being extremely cautious about who knew the exact nature of her illness. Much as I philosophically acknowledged her right to determine who knew, keeping a tight lid on the situation was growing beyond me. A few other people, including Jeff, the man I was living with, put puzzle pieces together without my technically violating a confidence; one or two discreet souls I told outright. They weren't people who were going to blab or bother her, and I was desperate for ears and shoulders myself.

The moments came more fast and furious as an eerie three-part invention of deterioration played out in the spring. First David called to say he was dying; treatments weren't working and he was leaving the hospital with an expectancy of two months, maybe six months max. Before I had the chance to reserve plane tickets for a good-bye visit, not 24 hours later, Elizabeth showed up in my office to bring up the same general topic. She had just been given test results showing a T-cell count of 36.[53] After years of weird maladies, misdiagnoses, and demeaning treatment by various HMO doctors, she leap-frogged all the usual stages of assimilating horrific news and displayed utter calm and relief. My being slid a few inches apart from my life while she discussed options (the most attractive being not doing anything) "I'm not afraid of dying; I'm a Buddhist!" she insisted. What she was feeling was anger, same as David – him for his body giving out, her at what she called the bureaucratic bullshit that lay ahead.

I cashed my frequent flyer mileage in for tickets to Seattle, but David proved his doctors wrong. He died within a week, two days before my flight.[54] I went anyway, as did several other friends from Houston, who

---

[53] The norm is in the thousands. Dropping below 200 commonly prompts people with AIDS to go on disability.

[54] He died in the presence of his partner, his favorite nephew, and a few neighbors, in his own bed looking onto Lake Washington and Mount Rainier. His lover told him his bags were packed; the train was at the station; get on the train; what was he waiting for? It was an Italian train, his partner marveled later. When the clock chimed 10, David left.

spent most of our time together looking at each other wondering what in the world we were doing there. I walked through the long weekend as if through molasses, disoriented by a terrific cold, prolonged sleep deprivation, and the strangeness of being in familiar surroundings with no hint of the person who had once made them so alive. I fell easy prey to pranks that toyed with my already fuzzy perception – failing to see that the rat caught in a trap near a basement shower was a rubber Archie McPhee product;[55] considering the possibility that David was the one who'd downed the martini we'd laid out before his photos.

His partner had barred all visitors from staying in the house – even David's mother, who hadn't come when his condition worsened but waited till after he died, to show up with her bags morning after morning on the doorstep (once, actually in the kitchen) of a man who was exhausted from devoting the previous month to full-time nursing of her son (not to mention from the all-night vigil before he died), and whom she expected to fix her drinks and take her sightseeing. She was told on three consecutive days to go away.

Night of the Living Dead

The man who would not be host asked me to stay, though, as his surrogate sister, on my last night in town. By the time dinner guests left and he let go a flood of tears on my shoulder, I had long since grown too tired to have any chance of falling asleep. He finally calmed enough to crawl into bed with his teddy bear, and I slid into agony. As night inched toward morning, I calculated the time back in Houston with each 15-minute chiming of

---

[55] Before slowly turning off the water in the shower, putting my clothes back on, and, summoning every ounce of calm and control, asking one of my hosts to help remove it.

the clock and succumbed to terror that an apparition of my dead friend would appear before me. "You wouldn't do anything to scare me, would you?" I begged silently, repeatedly, successfully.

How Long Has This Been Going On?

Back in Houston, a high school friend chirped over a car phone that he was on his way home from the hospital and that the tests came out fine. Hospital? Tests for what? While I was gone, his blood pressure had skyrocketed in response to the duties that had been "reassigned" to him after brutal corporate cutbacks a fortnight before. He was the second person from his office to be put in the hospital for an EKG.[56] I immediately issued an edict by email: no more deaths were to be allowed in the month of April; the matter would be open to renegotiation in May. All recipients complied; one even requested an immediate extension of his grant of immortality.

I started gulping B vitamins; Elizabeth started having migraines. She decided they were caused by a bad reaction to AZT, so she didn't refill the prescription when the first month ran out. She also gave up on the local support group for HIV+ women, without attending a meeting. Locating the group had put her through a labyrinth of phone calls (it's apparently one of the city's best-kept secrets), in the last of which the facilitator got angry with her for politely refusing to agree with assumptions about her

[56] Every cloud has its silver lining, and Bill's is a potently effective management tool. When people start lining up at his cubicle to bombard him with problems that aren't his, he uses the most grandiose of gestures to take out his blood pressure medicine, slap it on the desk, and pop a pill in front of the assembled throng. Asking "Do you *want* me to have a heart attack?" is just icing on the cake.

emotional state. She got antsy about being at the school[57] and began looking into alternative jobs for when the semester ended. She started taking days off, too, but her reasons weren't alarming. She was running errands; she was going to the doctor; her period was bothering her.

Ba-ba-ba-baby, You Ain't Seen Nothin' Yet

My brother diverted attention by chiming in, at 2 a.m., in the first week of May. He'd stumbled on proof that his wife intended to leave him for someone she'd seen only once, but had decided from email and phone conversations was her Ideal Man. The enthusiasm she'd shown for moving their family to another state for my brother's job change suddenly made sickening sense. Nothing else did, though. Daylight didn't shine any more clarity on the scenario, but it did bring my brother down the highway to my house for a weekend of incredulous conversation.

The morning after he left, Elizabeth called me at work for a ride to the emergency room. She didn't say why, and I didn't take the time to ask. I found her calmly filling out checks and deposit slips. She laughed at me for looking panicked; she was just dehydrated, she said, and methodically finished her tasks. The only thing disturbing about her appearance were fresh, enormous bruises across her legs. She'd fallen in the dark onto a coffee table she said her brother had moved into the middle of the room. She sent me to her car to find some insurance papers, which required rooting through the nuclear waste of fast food wrappers and leaking iced tea containers in the front seat, and had me feed the parrots and budgies.

---

[57] Especially after a distant friend left a loud, indiscreet message, on her work answering machine, claiming to have received psychic information that Elizabeth had AIDS and wanting to be sure she was aware she had it.

Then she asked me to wait while she went to the bathroom.

It took paramedics to get her out. She'd barely left the living room when a tremendous crash broke out. Giving the first clue that he was around, her brother called out to see whether she was okay. I found her zigzagged between the sink and the toilet and the tub, her eyes rolling back and her breath weirdly accelerating. While he called for an ambulance, I held her hand and silently chanted, "Please don't die please don't die."

What she was having was a seizure. She had another one on the examining table, which prompted the ER staff to rip off her clothes, never to be found. Before she was wheeled in for a brain scan that night, she stopped joking with me and a couple of other friends to toss off instructions for a will and powers of attorney.

Streptococcal meningitis, her doctor said the next morning, calling to confirm a no-resuscitate order Elizabeth had given verbally. A seizure during the night had nearly taken her out. I'd thought she had a year, a year and a half, maybe, but at least till the end of the summer. Every aspect of my being scurried to catch up with the truncated timeline. The doctor asked me to get all her legal papers signed up before noon.

We met the deadline, in the fastest document production of my career. It was also the first time I'd let anyone name me in a medical power of attorney. Before piling into the car with witnesses and a notary, I indulged in a panicked call to a wise, intuitive friend. "What do I need to do?" I begged. "Let her go," I was told.

There was still much to do in the process. The seizures were growing longer and more unnerving to witness, enveloping her in mid-conversation and spiriting her off to some eerie realm. She started complaining of hot flashes that consumed her entire body. She asked for ice packs and cold towels, and for help rolling from her back onto her side. By mid-afternoon, she lost any inclination to reach for the nurse's call button herself.

I got the job of spreading word to her friends and co-workers, most of whom had no idea she was the slightest bit ill. The majority responded with shock and concern and offers to call, visit, and help. The handful who got – or who figured out – the whole story were stunned, hurt, and puzzled that she had not told them herself before. A few – all practicing Buddhists – subjected me to the fate of the messenger, insisting on details and shrieking at me to stop when I complied, blowing up at me as they realized she'd withheld facts to which they presumed themselves entitled, furiously demanding explanations for her behavior and thinking that I firmly refused to second guess.

Whose Life Is This, Anyway?

The vehemence that one woman unleashed on me was explanation enough for Elizabeth's reluctance to grant her complete candor. I'd called her only because she was the one person who knew how to get in touch with the monk from their dharma center, Geshela, who was out of town for the week. She soon waltzed into the hospital room with a greeting that left us dumbstruck: Not to worry! Geshela had said Elizabeth wouldn't die before he got back to town! (Later in the week, she would outright tell Elizabeth that she *could* not die before Geshela returned.)

Death makes people weird, I learned long ago in my law practice. Now I was learning that dying has the same effect. The calls brought a parade of thunderstruck coworkers and the occasional patronizing Buddhist and New-Ager. A lot of the visitors had something to prove, and mostly it was that they were important to the person disintegrating in the bed. Some dropped by to claim reassurance, at times desperately, of their place in her ebbing life.

Still others were just plain flabbergasting. "You know you're dying, don't you?" Dharma Sister asked, brushing Elizabeth's hair. Later, after the patient shut her eyes, Dharma Sister brought up her opinion that Elizabeth needed to empower me to pursue claims against the HMO for misdiagnosis and malpractice. "In your unconscious state," she said, holding Elizabeth's arm, "You need to be thinking about the greater good that could be done by pursuing those claims." I shot her an it's-time-for-you-to-go-now look. She honored the message. When Elizabeth came to, I mentioned the conversation. "I know; I heard!" she exclaimed. "But what could I do? I was unconscious!"

Dharma Sister's rival in audacity was a woman who always began her phone calls to the room with an accusatory "Who is this?" and turned civil only when she heard my name. I met her in person mid-week when she interrupted my scurrying down the hallway to find a nurse. "The nurses won't give me any information," she complained. That's because they're not supposed to; you're not on the power of attorney. I asked her what she wanted to know. She wanted to know what was going on. I began an explanation. "I know she has AIDS!" she snapped, cutting me off.

What she really wanted to do was tell me two things. The first was that she'd connected telepathically with Elizabeth and learned that the hot flashes were clearing a past life when she was burned at the stake. I blinked. The second was that Elizabeth was going to the other side during seizures, and that every time we talked to her during one we were bringing her back and making it more difficult for her to cross over.

Oh, Yeah? Well, My Past Life Personality Can Beat Up Your Past Life Personality

Not trusting myself to say more, I thanked her abruptly and turned away. This present moment was hardly the time for past life information. What the hot flashes might mean on some useless esoteric level didn't do anyone any practical good; right now they meant we needed to put ice packs on Elizabeth.[58] The warning about interfering with her dying, on the other hand, made some sense. I wasn't about to say it out loud, though, and especially not to this woman.

Fortunately, these people were aberrations. Most visitors just wanted to spend some time with Elizabeth and do anything they could for her. The first two evenings turned into gigantic storytelling parties, full of laughter and tales of south-of-the-border travel. She was so coherent and interested that people didn't believe she was in danger – until her eyes would roll back and she would slip far, far away. And everyone would fall very, very quiet.

A core group alternated shifts at bedside (even overnight, a stint from which I unapologetically excused myself, due to how much of the days I was spending there). Maybe we were all in denial to varying extents, maybe we were sublimating emotion into the details of caretaking, but at least we were trying not to divert much attention from the main concern.

Her best friends, Ed and Heriberto, came by every evening and volunteered for the Procrustean couch (as did her otherwise largely absent brother). A police caseworker joined me in setting up practicalities, like a schedule of sitters and sign-in sheets for visitors. She displayed a willingness to stay that barely

---

[58] The flashes were a sign that her brain was losing the ability to regulate her temperature and was shutting down, warned a friend who'd put himself through a crash course in neurology after his mother's stroke a few years earlier.

cloaked an unwillingness to leave. Learning that she had recurring breast cancer put the ferociousness of her attachment into a new light: she was hell-bent on keeping death at bay. Jeff delayed his work days for morning stints, as did also Elizabeth's supervisor, who'd quietly stand watch, place a wet wash rag on her forehead, and never pry into why some of us always put on sterile gloves.

"Can I ask you a question?" became part of my greeting. As long as she felt comfortable answering questions, plenty kept coming up to which only she knew the answer. They weren't easy, but neither of us ducked them. Where was the safe deposit box? Did she want anything from home? (A tiny Buddha.) Did she want us to call her father? (After her death.) Did she want anything in particular done with her ashes? (Toss them into the water at Boca Chica, off South Padre Island.) Could we please tell her supervisor she had AIDS? (Again, after her death.)

When a social worker cleared the room on Day 3 to discuss a change in medication, the opportunity beckoned to finish a bit of remaining business in private. I asked the staffer to tell the people in the hall not to come back in until I let them. I'd already been able to tell Elizabeth I loved her. Now it was time to let go of her.

"You don't have to do anything for anybody," I stressed. "If you need to go, go. If you want to stay, we'll do anything in our power to fight for you. But don't hang on for any of us." It wasn't the overture to a prolonged conversation. Her response was succinct. "It's all so confusing," she said, almost whining.

She took her time sorting things out. Because she'd survived longer than expected, powers outside our influence decided to move her on Day 5 into a hospice in a converted apartment complex that used to house med students (and where, everything being connected, I'd visited a friend for a weekend 18 years earlier). Some latched on to this development as proof our friend would soon be home. I was brusquely doubtful. Maybe people did go home from hospices, but I'd never heard of it.

It sure defied probability when I got to the hospital that day. The pain had become so bad that she'd been crying during the night that she wanted to die. Her morphine, a nurse told me, had been cut in half. I launched a crusade to have the dose restored, which ran into the evening, thanks to the interruption of the move, and pushed my visit past the 10-hour mark and what little remained of my limits.

Before the paramedics arrived for the move, a hospice didn't seem to be the most likely place for her to be taken. Her agony was so palpable that I was sure she'd die before noon. I wasn't the only one. When Heriberto arrived to sit with her during his lunch hour, he lay beside her to caress her back and give her permission to die. I left them alone. Having spent the morning chanting the converse of my Monday afternoon plea, I berated myself in the waiting room for being so emotionally invested in her dying.

"It's not her time yet," he whispered on my return. It wouldn't be long, though; she'd told him she was getting on the bus.

Although two doctors had agreed to order it, the increased morphine dosage had still not been administered when I left the hospice at 7:30. When I looked in to say goodnight, Elizabeth had resorted to chanting mantras to evade the pain.

David's train had been Italian; Elizabeth's bus must have been Mexican. It took another day and a half to leave, not even 12 hours before Geshela arrived back in town. The last time I saw her alive, she was breathing mechanically, as if something were intermittently pumping bellows in her chest.

I watched for just a few minutes and left her in the care of others. A therapist friend had given me a ride, which I figured out, once my brain rested, was to make sure I didn't hang around, after the previous day's marathon had fried my circuits. He took me by a bookstore, where I saw a book on movies that I thought Elizabeth would like. Then I thought: I won't be going to any more movies with her. Then I thought: This is the first time I've had a thought that I'm going to have much, much more.

Her slow departure gave her brother another opportunity to spend the night in her presence, along with two old girlfriends who'd dashed in from other cities. One remarked that the room felt different in the morning, somehow peaceful and clear, as if something had been worked out during the night.

The call I'd been braced for all week came at 9 a.m. on Sunday, Mother's Day – in eerie symmetry with the likely cause, a blood transfusion after a miscarriage. I don't now know why, but Jeff and I went directly to the hospice. Elizabeth's body was strewn with flowers, a sight I'd seen only in 19th century Catholic photographs. Her brother was drinking coffee at her bedside, a pastime he interrupted to take Polaroids of her corpse. The other witnesses were sitting in the living room talking quietly. One of them, a co-worker of hers from years ago, mentioned something Elizabeth had done when she'd received the first diagnosis.

First diagnosis?

Yep; she'd told Nicky last fall that she'd been diagnosed HIV+. She hadn't told me this. I suddenly understood the shock and disorientation that other people had been communicating all week.

I got a little more when I phoned her supervisor to carry out her wish that he be told she'd had AIDS. He already knew; she'd told him on Tuesday, two days before she'd asked us to delay telling him till her death.

Incense and Reddened Necks

Ed found a funeral home willing to honor the Buddhists' requirements for handling her body, which had to be followed to ensure the proper transition of her soul. It was in Deer Park, of all places, the blue-collar refinery town where she'd worked. This home allowed her corpse to be laid out in the chapel on a daybed, underneath a tightly tucked Tibetan cloth strewn with bouquets and flower petals, next to a low altar blazing with white candles that Geshela lit during a prayer service.

At the funeral, a parade of speakers with stilted-metered, almost unintelligible Texas drawls talked of the dedicated, generous social worker they knew. Nobody mentioned mischievousness, or unparalleled intuition, or a passion for movies, science fiction, dowsing, UFOolgy, and *puta* red lipstick. Only her supervisor gave a hint of the person her friends knew; he read a poem urging survivors to grieve only briefly and return to their lives. Dharma Sister broke into tears saying that Elizabeth had best lived up to the Buddhist precept of treating all living beings with loving kindness and compassion. Jeff joked about taking the podium himself. "Elizabeth hasn't died; she's been kidnapped by aliens," he wanted to announce, or, alternatively, "Elizabeth had AIDS." The statements would have had the same impact on that audience.

All too soon thereafter I drove up to Dallas, since I wanted to see my niece and nephew before their parental soap opera relocated to separate homes in another state. We spent as perfect an evening as I have had with them, running around a fountain with dancing waters, playing with a menagerie of day-glo plastic ornaments supplied by a friendly restaurant bartender, batting toddler baseballs across a star-lit field. It was enormously disturbing. Their mother and I had been as close as sisters, and her acting so normal, so happy, and so affectionate under these circumstances made me queasy about what had passed between us over 16 years. Had that been real? Was this?

I fell apart, finally, at the end of May, after the long-distance marathon was safely over. It happened the morning my office Internet dial-up software stopped communicating with my modem while I was trying to meet an article deadline, for which I'd already received one extension. In the middle of prolonged, aggravating calls with technical support, I learned that my favorite aunt had just had a major stroke that would take away use of her dominant side and ravage a third of her brain. I held myself together long enough to drive to an office to pick up replacement software. On the return trip, the floodgates opened to tears and hysteria and screaming at God. Suddenly a weird awe overtook me. The world as I'd known it had disintegrated. How much stranger could this new one possibly get?

Don't Ask a Question Unless You're Willing to Hear the Answer

When the emotional dust settled, Jeff and I decided to take reign over some small portion of the chaos around us and hire a cleaning service for the house. I introduced myself to the employee before leaving for work. "My name's Kathy; what's yours?" I said.

"Marisol," she said.

I ran for it.

Tripping on the Time/Space Continuum

Doin' the Time Warp

Swept Away on a Musical Magic Carpet

I'm sitting in a sandwich shop having a serious discussion with a friend about his career when Seals & Crofts' "Summer Breeze" wafts over the loudspeakers. My attention drifts to the idyllic spring of my senior year in high school. Every cell in my body recalls the vibrant, anticipatory mood that fueled my existence then; I even see the empty auditorium stage where so many acts of mischief were committed. Then I realize an adult is talking. It's my friend who is, ironically, a musician. He's still in 1991. Whoops.

"Excuse me," I apologized. "I was being 17 years old."

This is not an isolated incident. Musical flashbacks are a recurring problem in my life. Some people have scents that trigger overpowering memories. My magic carpet is music.

Certain songs are inextricably linked with specific times and incidents in my life. Even just a few bars send me careening back through time. I'm helpless, jettisoned to the mercy of whatever level of emotional development existed when that particular trigger imprinted itself in my psyche.

For years, "Nights in White Satin" dispatched me to a senior-high body lock, more in love with life and endless possibilities than with any one boy, on the dance floor of the Petroleum Club in Dallas. Overexposure to oldies stations has put this particular time tunnel out of service. The retro playlists have yet to burn the bridge to a lot of other scenarios, though.

When Gene Pitney wails "It Hurts to Be in Love," I'm a child singing along in the back seat of a station wagon on the way home from my first trip to Six Flags Over Texas. No matter what the clock and calendar say, "We May Never Pass This Way Again" (again by Seals & Crofts; perhaps there's a key here...) is always Sunday night in college eating Canadian bacon pizza and playing finger hockey with ice from my root beer. Neither represents a level of maturity that I want to resurrect under normal circumstances.

The Small Faces' "Itchycoo Park" puts me back in bed in eighth grade with the bronchial infection that graduated me from pediatric medicines to antihistamines and the attendant burden of learning to swallow pills. (One peanut-butter-and-crushed-Dimetapp sandwich provided all the impetus I'd ever need.) The memory is strangely comforting, even on revisiting; I got waited on a lot and was even treated to my favorite teen magazine. Besides, the song is so rarely played that I don't go back there often.

Time traveling by music sounds like a cushy concept, one friend has commented. Not necessarily. Though the ride may be gentle, where I touch down isn't always pleasant. "One" by Three Dog Night brings back the adolescent memory of being moved a hemisphere away from my first big-time crush. More than two decades later, the song continues to arrest me; it was playing when I drove up to Whole Foods one night recently and I could not turn off the motor till the final chorus faded. Some part of me was still clutching her knees, huddled on a tiny bed, and heartsick for a little red-haired boy.

More dramatically, the Doobie Brothers' "Without Love" conjures flying glass and metal and a vehicle materializing in an intersection where none had been moments earlier. This one summons a level of bewilderment that jolts me even now. A college student falling into end-of-the-world hysterics is not the sort of thing an adult needs to have stirring in the back of her mind while attempting to carry on a mature conversation. Or drive a car.

The problem of subliminals is, I think, the major danger of this phenomenon. It's one that confronts my entire generation. We were brought up plugged into music. From the mid-60s, I used to go to sleep every night with a transistor radio playing against my ear, and popular music certainly shaped and controlled the culture of my high school.

And now that my section of the boom has aged into physical adulthood, we've dragged Our Music into the present right along with us. We won't give it up, and no one is pushing us to, anyway. It's played in grocery stores. It dominates entire radio stations. It's been co-opted by television commercials.

This omnipresence creates tremendous time-space confusion. Where are we? Who are we? What time is it, anyway? (Does anybody know what time it is? Does anybody really care? Not me; I'm a high school sophomore in an assembly watching a future gynecologist croon a Chicago song on stage, and as long as he's singing, I know I don't have to go back to class.)

The existential ramifications are enormous. Our psyches routinely splinter into different time periods, so the past constantly resurrects itself in the present. We never get a chance to bolt the door on the past or, more importantly, to permanently exit previous levels of emotional development. Our earlier selves are still running amok, and sometimes they scream for attention.

How can we steer the course of corporate America when surfing music is always pulling us back to dreams of carefree summers? Or make decisions affecting the lives of millions of people when some teenage version of ourselves is dancing away with abandon and exhilaration? Or govern the country when some part of us remains too young and lighthearted to take either life or ourselves seriously?

Come to think of it, maybe there's some hidden benefits to this phenomenon after all. Time warp, anyone?

Renegade Renaissance

For any visitors who somehow overlooked the rampant signs, the final Grand March of the Texas Renaissance Festival presented unmistakable evidence that something was amiss: The bagpipers leading the parade bleated out the theme song to *The Addams Family*.

"There's unrest in the kingdom this morning," cried out a barker. Was there ever. Period-costumed workers had given up any pretense of maintaining historical personae and assumed accents, normally so rigidly demanded of them, and abandoned their posts to pass gossip with a reckless lack of concern for being overheard. Attendance was slack in the aftermath of torrential rains, and the disoriented participants had the run of the grounds, through which they coursed in small clusters, dropping news and money on a sort of busman's holiday. What dampened many a mood for more than the rain was the slew of sackings and resignations that had punctuated the previous night. All emanated from King George, the sole shareholder of the corporation that owned the event and the true monarch in this realm, the person of Henry VIII walking on the grounds notwithstanding.

Each sector of the kingdom resonated with different information. The soothsayers reeled with the news that their sponsor had put their booths up for sale as a solution to growing tension between the king and the Esoteric Philosophy Center, as well as between the Center and the soothsayers. (They knew it was coming so they quit, someone pointed out; after all, they're psychics, right?) Some soothsayers called the Center and complained that they were being forced to do "oms," marveled the astrologer, clad in royal blue robe and peaked cap. Few appeared for work, even if scheduled; those who did spent the morning saying good-byes to and making purchases from favorite shopkeepers. (Not that any special impetus was needed to engage in shopping; by festival's end, my spending exceeded my earnings by a factor of three.)

A period costume provided the password to be let into any conversation. Two couples near the jousting field grumbled to your informant, a previously unknown soothsayer passing by, that some performers were sacked and the lady with the geese was reprimanded for, of all things, talking to other performers. Unthinkable that the inhabitants of this little village should get to know each other, said a man headed for the Royal Mint. "Lady Seer!" he called out. "Beware of kings dressed as puppets!" Rumor had it that King George had threatened to disguise himself in one of the festival's oversized puppets and spy on participants to catch them out of character.

A madrigal singer passed the word about the concessionaire of the Queen's Pantry, who'd been told not to return even though her staff had unfailingly opened early and politely to supply participants with coffee and

muffins. I trudged through the mud to visit the scene. As the wait-wench filled my mug with her finest wassail, I asked which of the pastries she could recommend. "None of them!" she snapped.

The ill mood was a quizzical cap to an odd experience. The Festival draws a peculiar work force that gives every impression of being sorely out of sync with the current calendar. Some of the participants are so suited to their festival personae that it is impossible to imagine them comfortably dressed in contemporary garb. Hair and beard lengths, exposure of flesh, and promiscuous flirtatiousness abound at levels that would be offensive and objectionable outside the compound. Somehow, over the seven-week run, a cohesive community develops among the historically clad, despite a constant undercurrent of ill will toward and from the ruling despot. (Many spend the tenure of the festival camping just outside the grounds, and their efforts to personalize the area result in several teeny-town touches – Christmas lights in the trees overhanging mobile homes and trailers, for example, or signs announcing the "Bizarre Bazaar" every Monday or "REN TV" at the Roadside Cafe on Saturday night.)

No matter whether overnighters, long-termers, or first-timers, we greet each other with, at the very least, broad smiles and genuflecting. I am initiated to the other extreme in my first few minutes on the grounds as a participant, when a long-haired, bearded, robed, and barefoot young man pleasantly reeking of bath soap envelopes my body. It's his morning ritual, he explains, introducing himself as Maniac the Monk. He hangs out with the barbarians, a semi-clad band of incredibly muscular men who brandish convincing, wide-bladed swords and camp next to the soothsayers in the Inner Circle – an anachronistic outpost of cars, pitched tents, and Port-O-Cans shielded by a ring of shop fronts and made invisible to paying visitors when its massive wooden gates are barred at 8:30 every morning. On my last weekend, I am finally made privy to a well-concealed doorway that affords a shortcut through the Circle to the far side of the grounds. This is a welcome development, since I have been running around the exterior of the Circle several times a day to cross paths with a friend in a madrigal group and flirt with an enticing chime maker. As I make my way from a Renaissance meadow, across a late 20th-century campground, and through the passageway back out into a Renaissance marketplace, I feel like I am slipping through centuries as well as geography.

My favorite character in the place is Ded Bob, a plumed-hatted skeleton puppet who is carried about in semi-fetal position by a human who goes by the name of Smuj and wears sackcloth draped across his face. Smuj's right arm goes up Bob's back, where he manipulates and sometimes removes the skull; his left hand holds Bob at the elbow, which makes for sweeping, fey arm movements. The main attraction is the Ded Bob Sho, in which Bob gets the audience to repeat or go along with just about anything he announces. The mood is taunting, impatient, and slightly menacing; the effect is side-splittingly hysterical. The point of the Sho is announcing its rules (which are written on sackcloth: Pay attention; Respond when requested; Respond only when requested) and punishing three audience members for infractions of the same. "Look into my eye sockets!" he commands the victims in succession, his skull leaning toward a human face. "Repeat after me: I've been Bobmotized. I am a Bob zombie." The trio is then menaced with a bonker (which looks like an atomic Tootsie Pop and triggers a series of Bob-commanded sound effects from the audience), put through a game of Bob Says, instructed to act out a playlet, and finally sent through the crowd gathering greenbacks for their master. ("I Been Bobmotized" t-shirts crop up mid-season – hot items that everyone wants but no one quite knows how to get.)

After my first Sho of the season, Ded Bob and Smuj take up the rear of the Grand March. "This is the dead end of the parade," he announces to the crowd. "Hey Bob!" one of my companions yells. "Your bones are showing!" The pair stops, the skull swivels in our direction, and Bob indulges in an uncharacteristically long pause. "Oh, never mind," he mutters, and Smuj carries him off.

Bob's antics outside the Sho are a frequent topic of discussion among participants. He takes to hanging out with the madrigal group – singing along (surprisingly nicely), conducting them with bony arm and gloved hand, calling one of the singers "Bagel Head" in deference to her cap, and even fishing in his own tip jar with his teeth and dropping money into their basket. The last weekend, word spreads quickly that both Bob and Smuj are clad in raincoats. I spy them near the ill-fated Queen's Pantry, both indeed wearing official TRF rain gear; Smuj's is white and Bob's is a child-sized purple. The sight makes me hop up and down with delight. In the final Grand March, Ded Bob once again takes up the rear, this time (still clad in purple plastic) peering out over the edge of the dead cart. "All hail Ded Bob!" the carrion carriers chant. "Hail Bob!" the complying onlookers reply, only it comes out more like "Hell Bob!" In mid-afternoon the sound of Bob wandering near the doorway of the soothsayers' booth distracts me and a pair of college students who'd just sat down for a reading. We run out to watch Bob taunting women. "Where have you been all my death?" he cries to a giggling young woman. "Oh, I'm mortified!" He extracts her name and urges her to look into his eye sockets and repeat the litany, which swells to include giving Bob permission to feel her up. She balks at the last line. He begins the litany again, and this time ends it with, "I'll give you a dollar to stop bothering me, Bob." Again she balks. He asks for a kiss and offers his cheek. As she leans forward, the skull twists around so her lips fall right on his bony mouth. "Hey everybody, Vicky is easy!" Bob starts yelling. She backs away giggling nervously while Bob moves on to his next target. I resolve to offer Smuj a reading, but he moves out of my area before I complete prior obligations.

The madrigal group figures in the best single anecdote that comes to my ears. Ten minutes before a set, one of the altos commits the seemingly benign act of going to the restroom. The toilet won't flush, so she pushes the handle down a second time – whereupon it breaks off in her hand and a current of water bursts from the pipe, blinds her, and pins her against the stall door. As the restroom floods, she somehow frees herself from the continuing torrent and begins tearing soaked clothing from her body, screaming all the while. Members of the group rush in (even men) and all peel off part of their own costumes to fashion a makeshift outfit for her. They begin the set on time. She stretches her soaked gown across a cooler atop her car; to anyone flying overhead it must look like a supine person. The rest room attendant eyes her cautiously from then on. I tell the singer she's experienced my younger sister's misunderstanding the title of a late-sixties National Educational Television series on silent films, *The Toy That Grew Up*, as *The Toilet Threw Up*.

Because of our low rank in the Festival's hierarchy, the soothsayers are permitted vast noncompliance with the unbelievably detailed, strict costuming requirements, and we indulge in wildly deviating behavior as well. (Since the proclaimed default accent, for those who can't mutter the King's English, is late 19th-century Cockney, we see no logical inconsistency in maintaining equally anachronistic modern speech.)

"Look into your future? Pay me money not to talk about your past?" is the slogan of choice of a large woman with a strong New Orleans accent. We're supposed to have barkers luring in customers, but business being slow this year, we take to hanging about the entryways to our booths and calling out to passersby ourselves. One barker is a blonde, high-cheekboned, self-proclaimed vixen who spends her shift downing tankards of Scarlett O'Haras (cranberry juice and Southern Comfort). Her vocal style – or perhaps her appearance – works more successful results than others. A bug-eyed young man with Pan horns takes the subliminal approach. He stares at people and points at our sign, or follows behind them whispering through cupped hands. Another man works a pair of Chinese medicine balls in his hand and yells out, "Come play with my balls! It's the only thing at the festival that's free!" Older men take more aggressive approaches.

"Spend money!" one guy yells belligerently. His counterpart in age engages in an equally repellent litany. "Read your stars? Your cards? Your palm? Past lives? Future lives? Do you have a life? Get a life!" I settle on, "Have your fortune told?" Amazing how many men feel compelled to answer that (a) they don't want to know or (b) they already know theirs and it's bad. When several of us lean in the arched doorway during slow spells, it feels like we're waiting for customers in the parlor of a whorehouse.

During one of those bouts of hanging around, Maniac the Monk walks by, this time wearing the gear of Robin Hood's Merry Men. He takes my greeting as an opportunity to lean his head into my breasts. "I'm not Maniac," he explains. "I'm his triplet Wesley."

Many of my comrades give me a more than slightly uneasy feeling (such as French-accented Sybil, who openly argues when visitors decline her offers of readings). By the last weekend, a few kindred spirits identify themselves. I tell a thin woman with braids and orange buckskin garb that I am a lawyer; she responds not with a double-take, as did the astrologer, but with the news that she is a tax accountant for Exxon. She discloses another unusual endeavor: "working the lines" at the airport, which means standing near the gate with torches and guiding planes to their parking places. The astrologer regales me with tales of his past-life research and documentation, through which he has uncovered tangible, historical evidence that confirms information received in some past life regressions. In the process he has discovered that astrological configurations, personalities, and handwriting carry over from life to life. A critical point in this realization was stumbling on the identical

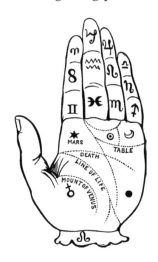

appearance of the handwriting of Mary Shelley and his partner, who is the reincarnation of the authoress. To test the idea they sent writing samples of both to handwriting analysts, all of whom confirmed that the writings came from the same person, though some 50 years apart. By the by, he mentions, Beethoven is currently teaching music to deaf children in Alabama. When we trade business cards, he glances at my palm. "You had the Egyptian initiation," he tells me. "Huh?" I respond. "See that Y at the base of your fate line?" he points out. "Actually, you've got two of them. You did it twice." I refrain from asking him what "it" entailed.

He intervenes on the last day in a conversation between me and the other male in the booth, a palm reader who has misinterpreted a facetious response of mine as disagreeing with something he said. The astrologer demands my birth data and looks in his ephemeris. "That's the problem," he says casually. "His Pluto opposes your sun. Sexual tension." "Okay, then, hold my hands," I say, thrusting them palms up at the reader, who proceeds to praise my intuitive abilities and break the news that I will have one … no, make that two children. "They gonna tell me who the father is?" I ask. "You'll know," he says.

Our booth is not the sole outcropping of sexual tension in this little compound. The muddy grounds veritably throb with the same. A bevy of wenches chant, "You can't beat our meat, but you can eat our meat!" Guess what they were selling … probably something on a stick. On the next-to-last eve, I stumble upon restroom graffiti: "The pewter guy is easy! Booth 19!" and below, in a different hand, "good and lots of fun!" I catch sight of him the next morning. He's middle-aged, balding, and significantly overweight, and gives no sign of a redeemingly great personality. The ol' s-tension erupts dramatically that last day when, in the waning afternoon, a harlot attacks a man outside the soothsayers' doorway. Harlots have been hired to wander the grounds armed with a tube of bright red lipstick, all the better for planting visible kisses. Hearts painted on each bulging breast, this harlot jumps at her victim, flings her arms around his neck, and wraps her legs around his groin. As they kiss, they fall to the ground, where she plants herself on top. He rolls himself on top of her; the crowd starts chanting rhythmically. A good 30 seconds later, she rolls back on top. His friends are photographing the event from a safe distance. When the couple finally breaks loose, everyone cheers wildly.

I depart our booth long before sunset and take my farewell of the grounds. At the gate, where the performers gather for the closing ceremony, I catch up with my madrigal pal, who has traded the bagel head for a red velvet cap. We pass a group of mud beggars seated on the ground, blowing out modern tunes on conch shells to the drum beat of the troll, a long-haired, silent blond man with face painted completely black, who has spent much of the festival crawling about a rope web strung high in the trees at the back of the grounds. We watch the king and his courtiers move through stately dances, which give way to frolicking polka-like steps and finally abate while the crowd sings the official closing song. During the song, a juggler takes the center of the circle and sends twirling fire batons into the trees. One almost glances a limb, and I regret its clean escape. A tree igniting would have been a fitting end.

The Tracks of My Years

I have a problem with cities I used to live in. Whenever I return, their geography no longer exists in time present for me. I don't see the streets and buildings and landscapes in just their current state; in my eyes, all are embellished with a dusty patina formed by layer after layer of memories.

Dallas, the city where I spent the years from second grade through college, was long a trigger for this phenomenon. A decade and a half of experiences, primarily adolescent, stockpiled the city's streets with associations that loomed as ineradicable. I'd nod figuratively to each on every visit home, as if acknowledging a revered but distant colleague, or reciting a litany of history.

Driving into town, I'd glance to the right at the lingerie store to which a bridal shower party abducted the guest of honor and subjected her to a communal purchase. On the left, I'd look up at the sign with the concentric lights that spiral in sequence to the center, the remains of a store that bore the surname of my fourth grade teacher. The sight of the bread factory would bring to mind a high school friend's claim that she sneaked a plastic hair clip into a vat of dough during a guided tour. The apartment complex just beyond would summon the eccentric English professor who used to live there, who didn't know how to drive a car, until he finally, and in short order, got a license, a car, and a house, and who once invited me in, after a ride home, to a living room with a grand piano topped with a red Mickey Mouse train set and, nearby on the floor, a towel and lubricant, from which we both averted our gaze.

Exiting the highway would only escalate the visitations. The route would pass the house of my little sister's first piano teacher, whose husband flirted with her in public (marital behavior I'd never seen before); then the house of the swimming coach whose confidence led to miraculous performances even in us nonathletic pupils; and the multi-story, lot-consuming behemoths built on what had been blocks of empty fields, where a spider bit my ankle and I looked up to watch a plane flying over head and was convinced it was the flight carrying the Beatles after their concert. A spectral dachshund with my brother's first name would always burst through a long-gone front door as I'd slow down in the approach to the family home. My car would stop along a curb that was once lined with redbud trees. Even after the front yard was cleared, I'd still see the mimosa tree that I climbed in my very first morning in that house (in an act that defied, and destroyed, day-old stitches in my knee) and that I jumped out of in a political statement to my Junior-Senior Prom date about the traitor-to-womanhood he'd invited to double-date with us.

And that was before getting to the door.

Whether by overexposure and desensitizing, or just plain growing up, I have somehow shut off this endless loop of apparitions and associations and dispatched them all to the quieter realm of memory only. The ghosts have faded from my sight, no longer lost souls trapped between the worlds. Their counterparts in Austin, where I spent three short, intense years in the personality-disorder inducing pressure-cooker of law school, have yet to move on from me. Around every corner in central Austin lurks testimony of the past, or maybe just a transit way to an earlier self.

I drive by Milto's Pizza Pub (or, more likely, I walk in and order a souvlaki sandwich), and timelines rife with laughter converge. It's simultaneously the Sunday night the owners of two natural food stores were sharing a pitcher of beer and casually violating antitrust laws by divulging, and fixing, prices for various products; and it's the June afternoon a neighbor and I should have been thrown out for laughing and screaming, having gone astray on a theoretically six-block walk that detoured wildly thanks to the influence of gin, which we'd been mixing with Dr Pepper once the tonic ran out; and it's the Saturday afternoon of a recruiting weekend, when the, shall we say, assertive wife of my supervisor flamboyantly removed her contacts and the pair (of humans) traded lenses and accusations of who had taken whose.

I stand in the wing of the law school that was under construction from my first semester on; my eyes see wide, pristine hallways, but my sensors perceive the doorway to the cluttered law review offices, the bulletin board on which grades were posted by social security number, the lobby to the library where I'd spend Saturdays reading assignments against the roar of football games from the stadium a few blocks away, or slip in after hours (exercising the privilege of law review that allowed chronic overachievers access to books at a time when any sane person would have been sleeping) and dance on a table in the Federal Room while singing, "We're the knights of the Round Table" from *Monty Python and the Holy Grail.*

A few of the Austin ghosts actually stir longing for their long-gone physical counterparts. I'm thinking especially of the Lone Star beer sign, R.I.P. – a two-footed metal tower, next to Conan's Pizza on the Drag, which had the time and temperature and an ad for guess which national brew of Texas across the top. The sign wasn't important for its appearance, but for its interactive delights, and for introducing virgins to them. Instructions would be issued with no explanation: Walk up to the sign. Turn your back to it. Bend your knee. Kick it back. At which point, if the hit was good, a shhh-t-t-t-t-t-t-t-t-t-t shot up the metal like a *Star Trek* sound effect. The reaction was always the same: absolute, unexpected, completely satisfied delight, followed by the impulse to show it to someone else.

While it can be sad to note the absence of treasured landmarks, it can be sobering to realize that current geography still lines up with ancient memory. When flooding closed the highway between Houston and Dallas at Christmas a few years ago, a detour took me and frequent road buddy John westward, to the north-south highway that links Austin and Dallas. When I drove this road in law school, I'd stop, on the way home for holidays, in a tiny Czech town outside of Waco to pick up a box of kolaches. Minutes on the highway reawakened the desire. Let's stop in West[59] and get kolaches, I suggested to John, who gave his usual assent to a scheme involving either unknown territory or food. I pointed out the exit, directed him onto the main street, and recognized the bakery on sight. I stomped in without hesitation, searched for the counter, and placed my order, at which point it hit me: I hadn't been in this place for 13 years. Nothing about it looked any different. And it hadn't occurred to me, till that moment, that it might not be there.

I've come to expect ghosts on the road. But now they're starting to rear their gauzy heads on my home turf. I've lived in Houston longer than in any other city, all of those years concentrated in a neighborhood spanning only a few miles. Memories are stacking up, and every now and then one slips out of the past and plops at my feet, or smacks me in the face, or slides out of my mouth and prompts me to unleash reminiscences on people who may well not want to hear them. Usually it takes a lingering emotional charge to merit the contact. I can pass Mykonos Greek Island, for example, without automatically thinking of the birthday dinner that drew 17 people (and so many packages that the waiters were tripping on them). I cannot, however, see the Dot Coffee Shop on I-45 South without remembering

---

[59] Note from the future: a town, not a direction.

how intensely I considered ramming my car into my brand new ex's brand new Honda in that parking lot almost a decade ago.

These being personal ghosts, they are not visible to others. When I clue a companion in to a visitation, I may well be paid back for yielding to the urge. One night last fall, on the way to a dance concert at Houston Community College, I was compelled to mention an audition on that campus last year for the local premiere of Stephen Sondheim's *Assassins*, at which I had perversely chosen to perform both parts of a scene from that show between Sara Jane Moore and Squeaky Fromme. (The ploy didn't work, but the look on the director's face when I identified the title made it – the preparation, and the agony of auditioning – all worthwhile.) Divine retribution is one explanation for the snowballing of worlds colliding that ensued.

The concert featured a former client, a dance company that I had incorporated 12 years earlier. The company's artistic director was, until recently, my next-door-neighbor. She would, just before curtain, take the seat in front of me during the concert.

Before the doors opened, I looked over the program and was surprised by a name on the cover. The company had just hired as its first administrative director the wife of the parochial school theater director who'd nearly lost his job in the late 80s because of me. (I'd rented his hall for a concert by performers I was sure he knew were gay, and the last-minute dispute that erupted when his bosses figured this out worked its way up to the Bishop and the Chancellor of the Diocese, and an out-of-court settlement that left the concert in place. That this woman still speaks to me at all, even if occasionally insultingly, is an amazement to me.)

A man in the entryway looked familiar; further study of the program uncovered his name – in the roster of the board of directors. He was another former client, a Harvard-educated lawyer who hired me for a will and is the only client ever to inquire into my educational background before deigning to hire me. A dancer's name looked familiar, too, and it took a good 30 minutes to realize that where I'd seen it before was in a will, and specifically the one of one certain Harvard-educated former client.

Inside the auditorium, I recognized a few people from the Unitarian church where I used to sing, and another couple from the United Church of Christ in whose choir I more recently sang, until repelled by the Lenten liturgy and the plight of being the only unpaid soloist. Several rows ahead I spied the two lawyers from whom I used to rent office space, the ones who changed the front door lock without telling me and hired their barely-English-speaking, only-weeks-in-the-west Chinese daughter-in-law to answer the phones, and who reacted with irritation when a skiing trip was disrupted by their secretary's suicide attempt. I immediately prayed for invisibility.

At intermission we discovered that the row behind us contained my companion's oldest friend, whom he has known since junior high. Her date was: the director of *Assassins*. The cloaking held; I went unrecognized.

The first failure of cloaking occurred during intermission, when I was approached, and spoken civilly to, by the parochial school theater director/husband of the dancer company's administrative director. The second failure thwarted my efforts to sneak out of the auditorium, but made my presence known only to the UCC couple (one of whom used to be, no coincidence here, a coworker of my friend Rex), who flagged me down for an explanation of why I wasn't singing for their congregation anymore.

"There are only 200 people on this planet," Rex says of the evening. Not just that; just about all of *me* was in one room. Having a multi-faceted existence works when all the facets behave and stay in their designated sectors. When they slide across borders and converge, the impact is unnerving. Throw in ghosts and past selves, and the experience gets too crowded for my comfort.

The evening's a portent, signaling that I have lived here too long. Soon there will be no room for the present, and the only option will be to move.

Or hire an exorcist.

You Can Run, But...

I Love a Parade!

Doo Dah, Doo Dah

The Doo Dah Parade in Ocean City, New Jersey is a celebration of imitation. The name and concept – basically, goofiness – certainly aren't original. They were lifted from the spectacle that's been going on for years in Pasadena, CA. The lift wasn't even direct; the Ocean City folks got the event by way of Pitman, NJ, which sponsored a Doo Dah parade for three years, until an erotic float slipped into the otherwise family-oriented line-up. Ocean City eventually put its own imprimatur on the parade by adding the fillip of an annual lifetime achievement award honoring a classic comedian. This little bit of fine-tuning drop-kicked the  copycat aspects of the event into all sorts of weird new territory as scads of fan clubs and impersonators, from the invited to the self-appointed, now crowd the festivities.

The parade I attended, which took place, as always, on the Saturday following April 15, bestowed the award on the Marx Brothers. Would-be Grouchos came out in droves; Groucho glasses were the single most common accoutrement in and alongside the parade route, the runner-up being oversize plastic cigars. He appeared in the company of Chico and Harpo in two convertibles, one of which was driven by a priest who would later torment the paying public with atrocious visual puns during the afternoon's comedy show.[60] The priest's set of the Brothers had the distinction of being the shortest and the cutest; they couldn't have been as old as 10.

The multiple Marxes were but the tip of the iceberg of disorientation that lumbered down the boardwalk. They paled in comparison to the lead-off posse of men, women, and children wearing raccoon-tail hats and chanting "Woo woo" without cracking a smile. I was mystified. "The Philadelphia chapter of the Order of Friendly Raccoons," a sign finally explained. Ah; *Honeymooners* fans. (Hey, not all portions of my Baby Boomer card are validated.) After them, things were relatively straightforward: Impersonators of long-dead comedians. Marching bands of varying levels of competence (including negligible), most playing "De Camptown Races," one sporting Groucho glasses. The other Spice Girls (including Old Spice, in a walker). Dogs in clothes.

And then there was Supergirl. In the parade, she was actually fun, running down the boardwalk with arms outstretched, then hopping on one boot to suggest flying. Later, when she accepted a piece of the boardwalk to honor her participating in the parade for 10 years, she radiated an unsettling seriousness that didn't exactly go hand-in-hand with portraying cartoon characters. Her long hair looked like it hadn't been washed for days; her equally less-than-cheery male companion could have come

---

[60] One did make me laugh: Shouting "The infantry!" at a baby doll. Otherwise the parade of props was along the lines of a picture of a sax on a TV screen. People were actually laughing. I hurt.

straight from a sci-fi con. That evening I would hear wondrously strange scuttlebutt from other participants: When she appeared as Underdog, she wore the same outfit as Supergirl, the only difference being that she called herself Underdog instead of Supergirl; she'd been on Howard Stern's show twice until she figured out he was making fun of her; the previous year, when someone asked her how Howard was, she went after the heckler with the club she was carrying as Spectrum the Ghost King.[61]

Groucho's older daughter, Miriam Allen, was supposed to be accepting the Brothers' lifetime achievement award, but slipped out of the parade before the convertible labeled with her name passed my vantage point. By the time I caught sight of her, she was on the reviewing stand. One comic impersonator after another joined her as the parade progressed. By the end, Laurel and a very spooky looking Hardy, Abbott and Costello, W.C. Fields, Mae West, Charlie Chaplin, Groucho, Harpo, Chico, and a second, pith-helmeted Groucho (talking to Miriam) were lined up, while an Elvis impersonator ripped into song in front of them. The collision of cultural iconography was head-spinning. I had to walk away.[62]

---

[61] She also got print attention that weekend. The Ocean City paper devoted an entire 11×17 page to an article about her that was one of the finest crafted pieces of journalism I've ever seen. The writer went overboard to draw absolutely no conclusions and attribute even the slightest subjective statement solely to Underdog Girl. She believes God compels each person to do whatever they do best; for her, that's portraying characters in parades, which she does along the Jersey Shore and environs; her portrayals are an art form arising from modern dance, which she gave up studying when a teacher misunderstood the groundbreaking work she was doing and insisted too much on "perfection;" she declines to reveal what she does for a living, but will disclose where she lives and that she travels by bus; Howard Stern is a devil who didn't bother getting the facts about her. The writing technique had the effect of making the author's attitude quite clear.

[62] This might have driven some people to drink, but they would have had to come prepared. Ocean City is dry. Unlike its notorious neighbor Atlantic City, it's a bastion of clean fun for the whole family.

I should have reacted the same way to the comedy show.

At one point I realized that the funniest thing I'd seen was the Abbott and Costello act, which was neither a good nor a comforting sign. (They were, however, dead on in their deliveries.) At another point I realized we were watching a red fox in a purple T-shirt finger-sync "Telstar" on a hand-held keyboard, while fellow non-cartoon-character animals cavorted, and a porcupine that looked like Don King axed chords across an electric guitar. When the formally dressed Eddie Cantor impersonator[63] returned, the exit cue grew too insistent to ignore any longer.

Disorientation continued into the evening, when we had dinner in a room full of impersonators out of makeup.[64] W.C. Fields ate with Abbott and Costello, who made a point of wiggling his appropriately chubby little fingers at me. An almost unrecognizably muscular Chaplin popped by their table. Mae West/Carmen Miranda sat with three attractive young men who gave her undivided attention. As the meal crunched to a close, the question buzzed through the room of who next year's parade should honor. Somebody mentioned Lucille Ball. Mae/Carmen immediately volunteered her services because she had the wig for the job.[65] At the end, a major Marx researcher showed a videotape of hilariously racy outtakes from Groucho's *You Bet Your Life*, and Miriam went to sleep.

[63] —who looked so unlike his model that I thought he was Vic Damone (the real one, not a Sears one) in the parade.

[64] Except for Abbott, whose mascara was still visible. Even from across the room. I'll complete the picture: he appeared to be around 60, artificially red-headed and – big surprise – gay.

[65] Six weeks later, I heard that this little interchange had taken; Lucy was the next honoree.

Coney Island Babies

My first Mermaid Parade at Coney Island (and the end of the 20th century) was as singular as the title suggests. It was full of filmy, iridescent fabric in stunning blues, greens, and purples; bikini tops fortified with scallop shells, fake pearls and glitter; and, of course, flesh. Lots of flesh.

One woman's top consisted solely of a pair of carefully positioned rubber lobsters, held in place by a cord around her rib cage that was detectable only because of the indentation it made into her skin. Another woman's bust was covered by nothing more than sloppy blue spokes of paint encircling her exposed nipples, which passed within inches of a policeman without incident. There were child mermaids, one sleeping in a tiny, old-fashioned carriage that made everyone coo; retired mermaids in wheelchairs equipped with Evian water drips; drag mermaids; slatternly mermaids; pre-Raphaelite mermaids; and dancing mermaids. Three teen-aged girls in white, winged jumpsuits, periodically froze into choreographed poses threatening the crowd with guns; they were, their sign said, Charlie's Angel Fish. Two mermaids screeched into tiny plastic cheerleading cones as they encircled an aged Odysseus, who was running between them with his arms tied behind his back around a pole.

Supergirl was there, too, only not in her red and blue leotard. She wasn't in a mermaid outfit, either, but in modern dance wear. And she wasn't really dancing, either, just holding her veil out and waving it up and down in alternating circles as she walked forward. Her hair still didn't look washed.

The most striking aspect of the event was the audience's behavior. As the parade approached our section of the boardwalk, they stepped out in front, not just ahead of fellow onlookers, but right into the path of the parade. Sightlines evaporated for those of us under 6' as a mob of humanity enveloped the parade so tightly that everyone had to move back to let a float pass. The same thing happened later on the street below, where I caught the end of the automotive portion of the parade, which hadn't come down the boardwalk. Nobody was standing on the curb, because it would have taken stilts to see over the crowd, which had pushed into the middle of the street from both sides. Every so often, a policeman would order folks to stand back, but even then the cars passing through the gauntlet had only a few inches clearance.

Somehow the mob rule fit the locale. Coney Island has its own standards of acceptability, quite apart from most of the rest of our increasingly homogenized nation. Only hints remain of the grandeur that once characterized this amusement capital: ornate maritime medallions atop a Spanish-style building with plastered-in archways; an imposing parachute tower, the ride apparatus of which was long ago dismantled; a massive roller coaster, the Thunderbolt,[66] overgrown with vines and fit for a García Márquez story. The less savory elements that have always been part of the area now dominate Coney Island. It still has freak shows, one established and large enough to occupy a building, which is draped with outrageous painted signs like the banners that used to cover carnival sideshows. This one has a connection with the local museum, which happens to be upstairs and was denying the public access to its treasures from long-gone parks, like a Steeplechase horse, so the freak people could use it as a dressing room.

The other freak shows are one trailer enterprises, the kind that make patently ridiculous claims to lure passers-by to hand over some money and walk up a tiny set of stairs to see whatever is really inside. The world's smallest horse ("Lilliputian among horse flesh!" crooned the tape-loop

[66] Note from the future: the Thunderbolt is now long gone, but Coney Island has since been enjoying a cultural and commercial revitalization.

barker) was around the corner from the world's smallest woman, to whom, it was claimed, you could actually talk while you peered down at her.

Next to her was a billboard claiming that a beautiful model had been decapitated in a car wreck and was being kept alive by medical science – just like one I'd seen at the 1972 State Fair of Texas, except that the date on the fake newspaper headline on this one had been painted over with "1985." Had I been a medical doctor carrying my credentials, I could have seen her for free. Since I wasn't, I passed up the chance to see if she was, in fact, obviously altered with mirrors, as friends who'd ponied up the fee in 1972 had reported.

The neighboring trailer was the most disturbing of all. As if enormous lettering on the billboard didn't convey the point, an over-amplified recording proclaimed the evils of drugs, which had left the person on display irreversibly brain damaged. Surely prolonged exposure to the insistence of the spiel was enough to do the same; I wondered what it was doing to the ticket seller. Eldorado Auto Skooters ("Disco Bumper Cars!") raised the same question. There must be a limit to how many times a person can hear "Bump – bump – bump yo' ass off!" and not be affected.

A carnival atmosphere was everywhere – in the streets, on the boardwalk, in the narrow, densely packed amusement parks, in the game-filled alleys, even in the appearance of people passing through. Tattoos were rampant, elaborate, attention-grabbing, skin-consuming works of art, across chests,

arms, calves, napes. One young woman – an otherwise perfectly middle class and extremely attractive young woman – had cuffs of flames circling her wrists, lapping at the backs of her hands and extending into her forearms. She was the most extreme of the women I saw with

gorgeous but prominent tattoos that amounted to a fairly unbreakable commitment to an alternative lifestyle. They certainly weren't likely to lead their bearers into most conventional ways of earning a living.

My favorite sight was tucked under the Wonder Wheel, in a cluster of coin-operated amusements: a fortune-telling automaton called Grandmother's Prophecies. She was a beaut. Her hair was white but her features were young and well formed. Her eyes were glass and eerie blue. She showed wear and tear from movement; one eyelid dropped half-way, and a small comb had fallen loose in her hair. One pointing finger was resting on a royal flush in spades. A spider, a fifth of spirits, and an electric candle were her other props. I had to see this in action. Between her and me stood a man and a woman listening intently while a young woman gave a Spanish translation of the card they had received from the machine. When they moved away, I put in my quarter. Her head moved. Her hand went back and forth over the cards. Her chest heaved in and out, up and down. A breathing mechanism! I was mesmerized. The Spanish-speaking man tapped my shoulder and pointed at the bottom of the machine. A card was waiting. I'd already got what I was after, but I took the card anyway. It didn't say anything about going to lots of parades.

Welcome Back, You Must Be Going

Gabe Kaplan doing a one-man show about Groucho Marx sounded like a good idea. After all, the former standup-comic-turned-pro-card-player peppered his 1970s sitcom *Welcome Back, Kotter* with nod after nod to the Marx Brothers.

So much for assumptions.

Part of the oddness radiated out from the location, an operation that debuted under the moniker the Sid Caesar Dinner Theater. Its advertising was strangely appropriate, giving off the faintly moth-eaten air that pervades such late career misfortunes of the Brothers Marx as *The Big Store*. Kaplan's colleagues in the first season line-up were the likes of Frank Gorshin, Lee Meriwether, and Mal Z. Lawrence. Kaplan may have the greatest – or most recent – fame, but they had it over him in the headshot reproduction department. His had the resolution of surveillance camera work, in the season brochure.

The theater didn't have its own space. Or even an outside sign. It consisted of a small elevated stage and a bunch of long communal tables in a ballroom at a special events center on Long Island – a once stately white clapboard mansion that had spawned two increasingly larger, stuccoed, boxlike additions. If a parking lot attendant hadn't told us to go to the back of the lot, who knows how long we would have spent wandering around corridors dotted with antique-looking furniture and lobbies filled with gargantuan chandeliers and maroon-carpeted walls decorated with gilt-framed paintings of flowers.

Kaplan opened with some well-targeted asides. "He's too tall! His nose is too big; his nose is too small. Well, for this afternoon, let's pretend that I'm Groucho and that this is a real theater." Alas, both illusions took a beating.

Kaplan was a surprisingly ineffective Groucho. No sense of cadence, or sentence melody, or inflection. He did work off the audience well (a couple hundred elderly Jewish people) (and a couple of goyim in the back) and throw in some good quips. Laying the groundwork for Groucho's placing his savings in the stock market (and facing ruin in the 1929 stock market crash), Kaplan tossed off, "I know what happens to actors who don't have any money. They end up in dinner theaters. The Jewish ones end up in kosher dinner theaters."

But he couldn't sing. He didn't even match pitches with the piano. Or stay in one key. His "Hello, I Must Be Going" was one long argument for pushing him off the stage. At the end, when he and the piano player and the utility actress (who played every female part) came out and launched into "Lydia, the Tattooed Lady," only the pianist's voice sailed through loud and clear, raising suspicions in my vicinity that Kaplan's body mic had been turned off. (According to *Newsday*, Kaplan acknowledged that he isn't "as good a singer" as Groucho, which is why this show was subtitled *A Life in Review*, rather than the usual *A Life in Revue*.)

So it was all the more surprising when, nearing the end, Kaplan sat at a dressing table with his back to the audience, changed his makeup, turned around, and – was 87-year-old Groucho. A ringer. Even more so once he opened his mouth. Old Groucho he can do – the phrasing, the sound of the voice, the mannerisms. Every bit. It was almost frightening.

A phrase that sums up the whole experience, actually. The cooling system was in overdrive. People were bundling up as best they could during the first act. During the intermission some people bolted, while others griped to anyone they could find. The bartender said the problem was in the hands of theater management, because the temperature was required by the performers' contract. An officious person was strutting around the place dodging kvetching, shivering elderly people. Instead of offering any kind of acknowledgment to the uprising at the head of our table, he barked something like, "We know! It's being taken care of!" and fled.

"For this amount of money, we could see a show on Broadway," a man announced from the head of my table. Maybe so, but would it have such a floor show?

When the show stopped, the kvetching didn't. It moved downstairs to the ladies' room. A woman with a cane groaned "I really have to go!" like a mantra, as she pushed her way up through the line when I was second from the front. Being the youngest person in the room, I decided to let her through, whereupon she tried to shove the woman at the front out of the way. "I really have to go!" "*I* really have to go!" they shouted back and forth. When they finally shuffled out and I was able to take refuge in a stall, the talk outside my door turned ugly. "First they poison us – then they freeze us – and they complain that we're unresponsive?" someone called out. Somebody else targeted Groucho. "He was an obnoxious man. His son wrote a book about him. It was an awful book. He was *poison* to his son!" There were widespread murmurs of approval.

Maybe the theater official knew something, after all. I followed his lead.

Groundhog Day

Punxsutawney was one of the first words my parents tried to teach me to say. It's the name of a tiny (and, until recent years, low-profile) Pennsylvania town that's made an annual ritual of forecasting the length of winter by consulting a groundhog named Phil. Whether this early exposure or the suggestive force of the name played a role or not, I have had a life-long affinity for groundhogs and, perhaps not coincidentally, for divination devices as well, though only the latter, for reasons of both practicality and inclination, has found expression in a compulsion to collect.

So when I moved back to the Northeast, it was only a matter of time until I made the pilgrimage to Groundhog Zero. The experience was enough for a lifetime.

Because the festivities start in the middle of the night, we drove in the day before, to a clean but soulless chain motel about 20 miles away, the closest lodgings I could find six weeks in advance, apart from rolling out a sleeping bag on the floor of a community center. A reconnaissance mission that afternoon to Center City (as Pennsylvanians call downtown) explained away the room scarcity – the town's two hotels are what you might call charmingly petite, and that's stretching it for one of them, at least as far as concepts of charm go. (There's a motel somewhere, too, but it's either of a Brigadoon-like character or lies off roads that exist in an alternate universe to published maps.)

The town bore about as much resemblance to the movie *Groundhog*

Day as the event would. The outer ring is strip center sprawl; within that, modest residences; within them, a business district heavy on turn-of-the-last-century brick buildings, and, at their center, a small, grassy park the size of a block. Gobbler's Knob is not in the thick of things, or even within strolling distance, but outside of town more than a mile away. The evening before, none of it showed any sign that it would be invaded within hours by thousands of people.

We set out the next morning before 4. Enough people had preceded us to drain the lobby's coffee pot. Although hours remained before the advertised Continental breakfast buffet, someone had laid out a loaf of white bread and stuck knives into opened jars of peanut butter and jelly.

Headlights trailed behind us as we bounded along a hilly two-lane road towards Punxy. The parking lot at the first shuttle bus stop was already filling with cars, and a human snake had already formed down the middle of a lane. A small trailer that might otherwise be used for fireworks was selling shuttle tickets for a buck apiece emblazoned with Phil's happy image. A parade of yellow school buses, helmed by middle-aged women, pulled in and, one by one, offered a good portion of shivering humanity refuge in seats sized for grade-schoolers.

To avoid being jostled, we headed for the last row – next to a man that we would have been able to hear at the front of the bus. He conversed with the man next to him, with friends and relations halfway up the bus, with his sister (who was celebrating her birthday, he advised all, repeatedly), with the stream of people who walked back and paid a level of attention to his thermos that suggested the nature of its contents and a factor in his obnoxiousness.

Blazing artificial lights greeted us as we stepped off the bus. A photo op awaited a few steps away, in front of a meteorological billboard with yet another happy depiction of Phil. Just beyond was an enormous, straw-covered, womb-shaped clearing surrounded by thick, tall clusters of trees. A row of remote radio booths lined the back. As we walked by, one announcer after the other gave a live weather report. It was 6 a.m., still 90 minutes till Phil time, but several thousand people had beaten us there, so we stayed near the back. Beyond them, on a stage at the other end, men in frock coats and top hats were jitterbugging to big band music. Off in the trees, an enormous bonfire was blazing, silhouetted by bodies running and dancing.

Top-hatted men yelled greetings at the crowd, college students took the stage to dance, people continued to pour and crowd into the clearing, a petite reporter stood on an equipment case to put her face in line with the stage and narrated the event into a camera, but none of the hokum mattered to me. Something primal was occurring. By the time fireworks shot through the trees and exploded on blackness, I was crying, without understanding or caring to know why. The snowfall that quickly followed was just icing on the cake, as far as the little girl within was concerned.

"What do you think about reports that they drug the groundhog?" demanded a college student who was taping interviews for a class project, he claimed. "With this many people, it's probably a good thing," I said. (The estimate from the stage was 9000; the next day's paper put it at 12,000. Or maybe it was 20,000. The numbers were enormous.)

Not long after I brushed him off, a procession of men in top hats filed down the middle of the gathering and assembled around a tree stump.

One man knocked on the stump with his cane. A door was opened and the woodchuck wrangler removed the guest of honor and conferred with him. Word came in the form of a long poem: He'd seen his shadow! Six more weeks of winter!

My companion immediately took issue with the pronouncement. It's impossible! The sky is gray! If he saw his shadow it was because of all the lights! This is – this is rigged! The outrage sounded genuine.

By 8, while crowds were lining up to have their photo taken with Phil, we boarded a bus back into town. This time we chose the middle, and ended up one row away from the loudest, yakkingest person on the bus, a college student who was immune to the torpor that was causing heads to nod around her, and who worked the announcement that it was her birthday into a monologue on the virtues of the malls of New Jersey. We jumped off at the first stop in town, where women and children stood so long in the line for the restroom at McDonald's that strangers started trading travel stories and itineraries, until the conversation shifted to the news break that the restroom had only one stall.

When I emerged, more news awaited: I'd missed the chance to have my photo taken with Punxsutawney Phil and Ronald McDonald. Two costumed Phils, with differently shaped heads, were working opposite sides of the street.

Months later, after we'd made a move that wasn't even in the realm of possibility that day, I looked up from a sink of dishes to the sight of something lumbering around the back yard. It was big and fat and furry and strangely familiar. A groundhog. I've seen it several times since, helping itself to apples, scurrying into one burrow entrance or another under the 30-year-old, weather-worn playhouse in the yard, even standing upright and breakfasting on the playhouse's porch.

It hasn't shown its face for months, but the neighborhood cats' continued interest in the playhouse makes me think it's still there. After the last heavy snowfall a week or two ago, the only tracks in the yard formed a straight shot to the main burrow entrance, where cats in transit like to stick their snouts.

I'll let you know if he comes out.

Halloween in the New Age

It was billed as a Harvest Festival, but the all-day shebang at a Chelsea public school on an October Saturday was really one big Halloween blow-out. The goodies table was stocked with lollipop-style cookies in the shapes of jack o' lanterns and black cats. The entryway, barricaded from the outside, contained a "pumpkin patch," a stockpile from which each child could choose one to decorate (not cut – no knives were to be found anywhere except by the frosting bowl on the cupcake decorating table). Overhead in the cafeteria, hallway and crafts area hung a parade of "Pumpkins for Peace," paintings of pumpkins emblazoned with American flags, or the World Trade Center towers, or yin-yang symbols (I counted four). "Booooooo" and "Follow Meeeeeee" signs hung from paper ghosts pointing the way to the haunted house, where a handmade "Scare-o-meter" lever lay in wait.

I was the roving fortune teller, the roving part of which I suggested without taking into account that my clientele would be two to three feet below my eye level. My rovings put me in the path of the other fortune teller on her arrival. She was to work in a tent; did I know where it was? I pointed to a round camping tent not four feet tall, festooned with gold bows, and two inflated pillows inside around a tiny round table. She froze, then laughed, then decided to be happy for a buffer against the wind.

My technique consisted of proffering a spread deck (the Inner Child Deck by Isha and Mark Lerner, carefully devoid of scary images) and asking anyone within earshot to pick a card. Two best friends started my day by interpreting whatever I said as applying to their cats, and sought me out again and again, together and one at a time, throughout the afternoon. I got the obligatory smart-aleck out of the way at the outset. The first boy I talked to took issue with my words. "That's not what it says," he said, "It says 'Six of Hearts!'"

Impossibly tiny girls picked portents of sharp, powerful minds. "Someone is watching over you; do you know who that could be?" I asked a largish girl dressed in a form-fitting white and pink fur something. She threw her head back and announced, "God!" The motion brought into sight a loosely hanging pink headpiece that identified her costume: a flamingo. "You need to stop being responsible and go on an adventure," I told one single mother, whereupon her companion doubled over, burst into hysterics, and offered to take the woman's child in for a few days.

A three-foot Buzz Lightyear didn't so much leap as repeatedly fling himself from the low stage in the auditorium. Two tyrannosaurus rexes emerged from the picnic table where their parents dressed them, only to topple over tail-heavy when they walked out into the cafeteria.

Closer to my eye level, a woman with a gold unicorn horn nodded me over to her. "You're real, aren't you?" she pronounced. After I described her card she summoned a pink Powerpuff Girl, who bounced around at the prospect of picking a card. "Wait a minute!" the unicorn commanded. "Find your center! Breathe, practice your zazen... now go to the one that speaks to you." Partway through my explanation of what the child drew, her attention jumped to some commotion elsewhere and she looked behind

her. "Focus!" her mother commanded. The child's head snapped back. I finished. Another girl asked if she could go next. As she reached out for the deck, the woman coached, "Find your center! Breathe....now, go to the one that speaks to you!"

Early in the day I saw a uniformed fireman rooting through a bin at the flea market out front. During the noon hour I  saw him march through the cafeteria, this time wearing face paint. As I readied to leave, he was wielding a mic on the front stairs and rhythmically exhorting the children dancing below. "Is Brooklyn in the house?" "NOOOO" "Is Staten Island in the house?" "NOOOOO" "Is Manhattan in the house?" "YE-E-E-E-E-E-SSSS!" He chanted hip hop lingo at them while they shook and jerked and jumped to the grooves. In between numbers he interviewed them about their moves. Then the music shifted. "It wouldn't be Halloween without – the Monster Mash!" he yelled. "Do the Frankenstein Shuffle! Do the Mummy Mango!" The crowd thinned. He ran down the stairs and stuck the mic out urging kids to howl.

"OOOoooooOOOOOOO!" "Yowwwwwwwwwwwwww!"

"ooooooOOOOOOooooOOOO!" A plaintive voice rose above the din.

"Can we have the hip hop back?"

They did. The kids came back.

An Unexpected Fit

T*he New Yorker* said the bra fitter there was one of the best, so I trekked to Orchard Street Corset on the Lower East Side. Most of the other stores on the street spill their wares onto the sidewalk, but not this one. When I opened the ancient door, I got a flash of the strange old shop run by the woman with barley sugar fingers, in one of the *Mary Poppins* books. The side walls were lined, floor to ceiling, with shelves broken into short, wide compartments. Each of them held a stack of wide, short boxes, most of which had lids askew and most of which looked decades old. A long, age-worn counter stood in front of the wall to my left. Behind me, on a chair by the door, a TV set was on, facing the counter.

The magazine's description gave me the image of a no-nonsense woman of advanced years, but the only person I saw in the shot-gun store was a tall, bearded, mouth-breathing man with frizzy red hair spilling out from under a yarmulke, an enormous gut (in an even more ample white dress shirt) spilling over black dress trousers, and a small black vest that was a good foot away from ever being fastened.

"Is your bra fitter in?" I asked.

"Yes," he answered. He looked at me. I looked around.

"What size you need?" he asked. I blurted a guess. "No," he said definitively, shaking his head. "Put down your purse." He lumbered towards me and put his palms below my clavicles and across my ribs, front and back, in rapid, practiced movements. He announced a figure two sizes smaller and began rummaging through boxes on the shelves.

"Come here," he said and led me past the counter. He handed me a bra and pulled a curtain between us. "Try this," he said. "You got it hooked yet?" he asked before I was halfway to that stage in the process. When I said it was okay, he pulled back the curtain, took a look, and frowned. "Try this," he said, handing me another, then pulling the curtain. While I was attempting to make the switch, a hand with another few offerings poked around the curtain.

As I tried on the bras, I became aware that a young black woman was checking stock and making notations on a clipboard behind me, in the back of the store. She acted as if I were invisible, so I paid her no further mind. Another woman soon joined me from the front, a slender, nicely made up young white woman wearing a black trench coat and an auburn pageboy wig. Without introducing herself or explaining, she took over, rejecting bras, calling out instructions to the man behind the curtain, and handing me new ones to try. From their appearances, these were not two people that would have occupied the same intersection of any Venn diagram that I could think of.

I heard the shop door open. "Do you have a Merry Widow in a 32A?" a male voice asked. "Strapless only," said the shopkeeper. The customer left. The shopkeeper poked his head around the curtain and handed me a white bra. "Try this," he urged. "It's cotton. For summer." He went away. The door opened and closed again. "Is it black?" the same male voice asked. "No. White," the shopkeeper answered. The door opened and closed. I gathered my choices (a good size smaller than his

estimate!), arranged my clothes, and headed for the counter.

The man gave me a look suggesting that buying four bras was shockingly extravagant behavior. The woman in the trench coat simply smiled. While she was tallying my purchases, a man in a suit walked in. "You do have a Merry Widow in a 32A?" he asked. It was the same voice. "Strapless only," answered the man. "Can I see it?" the other customer asked. While the shopkeeper dug it out, he told the man about how they were updating their website. I signed the charge slip and returned to the outside world. It still looked the same, so I headed home.

What Was That?

Sometimes, life's little mysteries do get solved, if you wait long enough.

I'm standing on a subway platform in Manhattan's financial district one Thursday evening about 8, long after rush hour has subsided, when an enigma lumbers down the track and grinds to a halt. It's a short train of unmarked yellow cars, all but one of which are completely enclosed, like pieces from some giant's Lionel set. Only one car, near the middle, has a window, a long, short rectangle above my eye level. The inside of the car is well-lit: I can see the top of a cluttered bulletin board and, occasionally, the top of a couple of heads. A train-robbing scene from *Butch Cassidy and the Sundance Kid* comes to mind.

I look inquisitively at my companion, who's lived in Manhattan for two decades. He has no idea what's inside. A door opens. An overweight white-haired guy steps out far enough to make his accessory visible to all: a gun and holster. He looks both ways, steps back inside and closes the door. Tops of heads move about in the window. Prisoners, maybe? my friend suggests.

I tell my companion about a service that my personal life commentator Rex and I wished for years ago. Wouldn't it be great if there were a phone number you could call and ask, "What was that?" The "What Was That?" operator would explain all manner of urban mysteries, from big booming noises to why traffic backed up on the freeway and then cleared, for no visible reason, to what the helicopter was doing circling my apartment complex for 30 minutes the night before.

This time I get my wish. "It's the money train!" a man exclaims at the other end of the platform. "It's the money train!" he yells, gesticulating to his female companion with movements that border on modern dance. "Look, it's the money train!"

The doors open again, and this time a parade pours out. Two by two they come, all identically dressed, not in prison garb but light blue shirts, dark blue pants and holsters. Big, heavy pistol-packing holsters. The people peel off in both directions and disappear from view, the doors close and the mystery train moves on.

Our train arrives. After we sit down and the train begins moving, a familiar voice rings from the far end of the car. "It was the money train! We saw the money train!"

Time and Space Warping at the Whitney

I never know when it will happen. One minute I'm immersed in one normal (for me) activity or another, and the next I'm hurtling through an inter-dimensional warp in the fabric of time and space.

My most recent trip happened on a Friday evening in the atrium that houses the cafe at the Whitney Museum, which had been cleared of tables and seating. I was standing at the back of a throng of bodies packed sardine-like in a semi-circle around the performers – Javelin, which was two men and stacks of painted boomboxes, and War Paint, a hard-driving, all-woman quartet that deployed the more traditional gear of electric guitars and drum kit. The sound from both groups was multi-textured and trance-like, which had the crowd simulating Brownian motion without anyone straying more than an inch or so from his claimed spot of floor. Even the sound guy was dancing. When his movement caught my eye, I noticed his age, and the warping commenced.

He looked older than I. So did the security guards. Ah. So what if I was pushing the upper end of the age spectrum; I wasn't defining it. My thoughts turned to the first time I realized that I was the oldest person in a room, when I was all of 27, at a concert by the The Judy's, at a club called #s on lowest Westheimer in Houston.[67] I glanced at my companion, with whom I have a history of trolling performance spaces on both sides of the stage for more years than either one of us easily owns up to. Once one of us had run a cassette recorder during a set of Richard Thompson's from the safety of a very large opened purse; now people all around us were brazenly holding up video cameras and cell phones to capture the performance. She showed no sign of paying any attention to age; instead, she was happily dancing in her own personal radius.

A man with silver-streaked hair and an unlined face stepped in front of me. The room teemed with taut bodies, long hair pinned up off the neck, weirdly beautiful tattoos (something shaped like a talcum powder container pouring stick figures down a woman's upper arm), and the occasional retro fashion touch, like a Don Draperesque hat. On the ground level above, visible through the glass that makes up the front wall, a line of would-be audience members, hoping to trade the cool evening breeze for claustrophobic conditions within, snaked from the entrance, along the sidewalk, and around the corner. My eye caught a man who had wedged himself into the tiny overhanging corner of the mezzanine. Trim build, sandy-colored hair with long bangs falling across his forehead, large glasses, and familiar face — it was my high school friend Doug, 11 years in the grave and now intently pointing a camera at the musicians below.

Earlier in the week, a friend on vacation had joked about seeing so many familiar faces walking around the streets of Buenos Aires. Her crack had set me thinking about the brain's knack for taking a quick look at a

[67] If you missed – or miss – this minimalist New Wave trio, look for videos of a live performance of the song that won it cult fame, "Guyana Punch."

person and fleshing out the features into someone it knows, a phenomenon that first happened to me early in my time living in Germany during ninth grade, when a girl walking toward me in the hallway briefly turned into my best friend from third grade. The man in the overhang, though, was no such replication. It was Doug from a parallel dimension, without the shortness of breath, without the reddened face, without the withering, without the lung damage that shrank his world for decades and ultimately shut down his organs. The last time we'd talked, I'd offered to bi-locate to a house-warming party he was throwing and hover over a tray of his home-baked muffins, a notion that amused him enough to mention it to party guests (which I know because one of whom told me about it when I called to pass on the news of his death). Now he was hovering over me. I kept looking, and his features stayed as static as his demeanor. He didn't dance; he didn't bob; he didn't move; he didn't smile; he didn't look around. Like the angels in the movie *Wings of Desire*, he was perched above the action as observer and overseer, documenting the event for purposes I could guess but would never know.

The more things change, the more they stay the same. Doug was the person who told me the French translation of that phrase, which his life ended up demonstrating. No matter how his circumstances and body shifted and declined, he remained immovably hard-headed, a verbal gymnast, and an observer of life from the sidelines. Where he's watching it still, while I continue to slide through time, space, and an increasing stockpile of memories and associations. *Plus ça change, plus c'est la même chose.*

Image credits

Author's collection: pages 133, 140, 145.

Dover Electronic Clip Art Series: *The Art of Food & Wine*: front cover and sectional frontispieces; Carbaga, Leslie & Marcie McKinnon, *Lively Advertising Cuts of the Twenties and Thirties*: pages 24, 237; *Women Illustrations*: pages 16, 32, 237.

Dover Pictorial Archive Series: Cabarga, Leslie, *Popular Advertising Cuts of the Twenties and Thirties*: page 202; Grafton, Carol Belanger, *1001 Spot Illustrations of the Lively Twenties*: pages 67, 70, 153, 159, 167, 168, 172, 220, 242, 267.

Illustrations by Noah Diamond: pages 113, 120, 128.

Pixabay: pages 26, 28, 29, 40, 41, 44, 49, 51, 55, 61, 64, 76, 82, 88, 92, 96, 103, 105, 111, 136, 156, 169, 176, 180, 189, 197, 203, 211, 217, 224, 229, 247, 255, 261, 274, 280, 281, 284, 289.

Acknowledgments

Thanks to Lisa Gray, my greatest champion among editors, and to Rex Gillit, David Opheim, Bill Griffith, Kelley Loftus, Reverend Jeffrey, and all the individuals behind the cloak of nicknames, for bearing witness to and helping me process so much of the behavior captured in these pages. The *Amore* interview would not exist without Jo Ann LeQuang and Patricia Taylor, whose ongoing conversations with me returned repeatedly to the puzzle of post-modern dating. I am especially grateful to Candi Strecker for supplying issues of the *Compendium* that strayed from my archives, and to Richard Pearson for his generous technical wizardry, transforming scans of publications into electronically editable form. I am indebted to Lefty Lucy for careful copyediting and a contemporary perspective. And I am eternally grateful to Noah Diamond for his graceful book design and even more for his long standing friendship and support.

About the Author

Since childhood, Kathy Biehl has scribbled down observations of human behavior and attempted to make sense of it. She gave up writing fiction long ago. A decades-long freelancer for mainstream periodicals, Kathy gained national underground renown in the 1990s as the publisher, Editrix, and main voice of the social commentary zine *Ladies' Fetish & Taboo Society Compendium of Urban Anthropology*. She has co-authored or contributed to guides on legal Internet research, dining, and personal empowerment. Her anthology *Eat, Drink & Be Wary: Cautionary Tales* was shortlisted for the 2022 Eric Hoffer Award Grand Prize. Her writing has also won awards from the Association of Food Journalists, Houston Press Club, and *Texas Bar Journal*.